W9-DBC-732

God's Plan to Reach the World: Acts 1:8

A Strategy for Individuals, Churches and Associations of Churches

SECOND PRINTING

C. Michael Gravette

God's Plan to Reach the World: Acts 1:8

*A Strategy for
Individuals, Churches and
Associations of Churches*

C. Michael Gravette

Copyright © 2004
All Rights Reserved

PUBLISHED BY:
BRENTWOOD CHRISTIAN PRESS
4000 BEALLWOOD AVENUE
COLUMBUS, GEORGIA 31904

DEDICATION

To Sarah Mitchell and other
Georgia Baptist Volunteers on mission,
who make a difference.

ACKNOWLEDGEMENTS

A very special thanks to my colleagues who's input into this book was refreshing, creative and extremely helpful.

Special thanks to Dr. Terrell Ruis for his special contributions.

Barbara Curnutt, Executive Director of Georgia Baptist WMU, has contributed a chapter on Acts 1:8 Education Strategy. Barbara leads our WMU with great competence and excitement. I appreciate her contribution greatly.

Dr. Mike Minnix, Vice-President of Evangelization for the Georgia Baptist Convention, has contributed a chapter on Acts 1:8 Evangelism Strategy. This chapter will whet your appetite for more.

Jim Millirons is Specialist for New Work, for the Georgia Baptist Convention. He leads the way in creative thinking for New Work Strategies. He has contributed a thought provoking chapter of Acts 1:8 Strategy for Church Starts.

This book is meant to provide Georgia Baptists, in particular, and Christians in general, with a strategy to engage in God's plan.

CONTACT INFORMATION

bcurnutt@gabaptist.org
mminnix@gabaptist.org
jmillirons@gabaptist.org
mgravette@gabaptist.org

Sign up to accept the Acts 1:8 Challenge at
www.gabaptist.org.
Look for the Acts 1:8 logo and click-in.

CONTENTS

CHAPTER 1

STRATEGY OF ACTS 1:8

Throughout history men have claimed to have been visited by God, or gods, in person, in visions, and in dreams. Outside of Holy Scripture it would be hard to discern the true testimony of these visions. One such vision was experienced by Constantine, the Great Emperor of Rome, and the first Emperor of the Holy Roman Empire. Constantine had been raised to worship many gods, which was the condition of many of the Romans. His special favorite was the sun god.

After becoming co-emperor of the Roman Empire he was about to engage in a great battle. Even though he knew that his army was superior to the enemy, he still sought help from outside himself and his army. He was said to be in deep thought about which god to seek assistance from. He remembered that those who worshiped many gods had often failed in battle. While he was meditating on whom he would serve, he called upon God (gods) to show Himself to confirm the true God. While he was thus seeking, there suddenly appeared above the sun a cross with the words, "Conquer by this." Both Constantine and his army were astonished by this sign they saw.

That night God appeared to him as he slept and spoke to him concerning Christ. From that day he chose to serve only God and His Son, Jesus Christ, and made the cross and the Latin letters XP (the first letters of Christ) the sign of his reign. This life changing experience set Constantine on a new course. As exciting as his conversion testimony, and others like his, may be, there is a greater, surer vision to build your life upon. That vision is the Biblical vision of the Word of God.

One such foundational vision, or plan of God, is Acts 1:8. This is God's plan to reach the world in the name of Jesus Christ.

Everyone needs to have a plan to enable him to accomplish the Acts 1:8 vision. A wise man once said (and many have quoted him), "To fail to plan is to plan to fail."

As soon as we begin planning, do we not negate the work of the Holy Spirit? Is not revival and reaching people the direct result of God?

God has a plan, and God is working His plan. Our job is to discover God's plan and plug into it. Acts 1:8 is His vision, and therefore our plan must plug into His vision.

Step one in God's plan is that every Christian is to be mobilized to get involved in God's service.

God's will is for every Christian to be On Mission for Him. The task of winning the world is not impossible if every Christian gets involved. There is no doubt that this is God's plan. Will it ever happen? Probably not, but that is God's plan. Even Jesus lost one disciple–Judas. He proved by his actions that he was never one of the disciples, but he was, indeed, lost to the cause. Does this mean that God's plan is flawed from the first? No, it just means that there is the standard that God will hold us all accountable to.

Mike Shula, the head football coach for the University of Alabama Crimson Tide, says his goal each year is to put his twenty-two best players on the field each game. That means he might have to move players from one position to a different position. Many coaches share this philosophy, but what happens when one of the twenty-two best players gets hurt? Do you scrap your plan? Do you forfeit the game? Of course not. You send in your next best player and continue the game. Can you win a game without the best players on the field? Absolutely. In fact, sometimes the team is actually better when substitutes are in the game. They bring excitement and enthusiasm that sometimes others do not have. They may not run as fast, but they are steady and dependable.

Therefore, God wants and expects the full team to show up, but He will work His plan with whomever He has willing and available. The good news for me is that God uses those who are willing.

Peter was able to walk on water (Matthew 14:22-33), not because of his talent for walking on water (he had never done it before); nor because of his great spiritual advantage over the other disciples. Peter walked on the water because he was willing to step out of the boat. I am convinced that any one, or all of the disciples, could have walked on the water, but only Peter was willing.

God also uses the available. Sometimes blessings come just because you have made yourself available.

Way back when Gerald Ford was President of the United States, he was scheduled to speak at the Southern Baptist Convention when it was meeting in Norfolk, Virginia, just a short distance from Washington, D.C. We had some car trouble driving in from Missouri, so we were running a little late. When I checked in for registration, I was told all the tickets to hear President Ford had been given out, but there was an overflow building not too far away where I could view him on the "Big Screen" projection.

I had never had the privilege of meeting or seeing in person a sitting President, so I was obviously disappointed. I decided to go to the Main Convention Hall, just in case I might see the President as he went in or went out. When I arrived, everyone had already been seated, and there was literally no one outside the building but me. After I had been there for about ten minutes, two men dressed in black suits approached me. They were from the Secret Service. They asked if I was a registered messenger, and I told them, "Yes." They said that the President was about to speak, but there were a few empty chairs on the front row that would not look good on TV. Would I like to sit there and hear the President? I was excited to accept the invitation. They escorted me to the front row just in time to stand for the President's entrance.

Because I had made myself available, I received a blessing. God will bless and use those who simply make themselves available to be used.

9

Likewise, the New Testament records the accounts of many people who were healed simply because they made themselves available where Jesus was teaching. God wants to use you, so just make yourself available, and be willing to do what He says.

Start where you are. This is your Jerusalem. It could be your neighborhood, church field, or city. You are where you are according to God's plan. It is no accident that you are in the exact place that you live. So, start "On Mission" right there. Acts 1:8 says "...first in Jerusalem..."

One observation I have made after thirty-plus years as a pastor is that some Christians will go on mission trips somewhere else, but will not be active witnesses near their own home. "First in Jerusalem" is the command. We must develop a plan to reach our city for Jesus—one convert at a time. Some wise fellow once quipped, "For me to love the people of the world is really no chore. My problem, it seems, is the man living next door!"

We will develop a strategy for reaching your Jerusalem in a later chapter, but first we have to accept the fact that God has charged each of us to have a vision for our city. As spiritual leaders, we must develop a vision for our city so that we might cast the vision to others in the church. We must accept no excuses and offer no reasons to not reach our city. Failure to plan and actively strive to share the Gospel in our city is failure of the Acts 1:8 command. It simply is not acceptable.

"But we've tried," you say. Well, try some more. Never give in, never give up, and never shut down your testimony to your neighbors.

I once pastored a First Baptist Church in a small and declining city in Alabama. It was one of those churches where you would pay $100.00 for a visitor! The people of this First Baptist Church were aggressive to visit any newcomer. In fact, during the two and one-half years of my pastorate, I never got to be the first one to visit a newcomer. By the time I found out they had moved in, four or five of our members had already visited them and invited them to our church. While I was there in this town of 2000 people, and decreasing, we were able to do two great things.

First, we caught a vision to grow, and we grew from 136 to 230 in average Sunday School attendance. Second, we had a vision to share the Gospel with every person in our town. We actually touched every single household, once a year for a total of three times while I was pastor. We shared the Gospel in every home. When God moved me from there, I could walk away rejoicing that I knew everyone in our little town had heard the Gospel and been given the opportunity to accept Christ. We had a vision–an Acts 1:8 vision — and we set a plan to get it done.

Now when I pastored in Dallas, Texas, several years later, the small town vision had to be modified, but God gave us a Texas-sized vision there.

Next, have a vision and a plan to reach your Judea. This would be your state of residence. When you venture away from your church field, you will encounter opposition. It is inevitable, but do not become discouraged.

In each of my pastorates there were individuals like D.J. D.J. was an older deacon, very active in the church, but never involved in faithful witnessing. His wife was a mission jewel, but it never seemed to rub off on D.J. Anytime I brought up going on a mission trip out of town I could always count on D.J. to make one of those comments, "Preacher, we spend too much going, and not enough doing locally." Or "Preacher, we need to keep that money right here in the community." (Remember Judas in John 12:1-8?) Or–"When God wants to save them people, He will." Or "Let's just do our work right here and quit worrying about other places." D.J. never led anyone to Christ that I know of, but he is in every church, trying to pour cold water on Acts 1:8.

We are losing our states. Last year in Georgia we baptized 33,000 people, which represents about a 6% growth. However, the population grew about 26%. We must reverse that trend and get a new vision and plan for Judea. Our Judea desperately needs Jesus. Even though we have 36,000 Southern Baptist churches and 16 million members, we are losing our battle with the world.

Those people in the next town, county, or mega- city in your state need to hear about Jesus. First comes the command (Acts

1:8), then the vision, and then the plan to accomplish it. Do you currently have a vision to reach your state for Jesus? Do you have a plan? Are you actively and aggressively working that plan?

The next area in God's Plan in Acts 1:8 is "Samaria." Samaria represents to us the U.S.A. Whoa! That is too much to digest: too many people, too great a need, and not enough time. If that is your vision, we are doomed to fail. There are millions upon millions of people in the United States, and it is impossible to reach them all.

"Impossible" means "cannot be done." The scriptures say, "With men this is impossible, but nothing is impossible for God." (Matthew 19:26)

Someone else might well say, "Well, yes, of course, God can do anything. Everyone knows that, but it is too much for one to do." It was God who, through Jesus, gave us the command of Acts 1:8. It was His command and His plan outlined in the verse, and He also said He would empower us by the Spirit to do the impossible task. He does not expect, nor does He want, us to attempt this task without Him and His power. "But," you cry, "How?"

Get a vision and God will supply the plan.

As you know, the next area of the vision is "...the uttermost parts of the earth." That is simply everywhere else outside the United States. Talk about a leap of faith and a God-sized task. Just getting to each country is chore enough, much less getting the gospel to everyone. Sometimes the sheer magnitude intimidates us, but again, remember that God is not intimidated.

A few years ago evangelist Billy Graham had an awesome vision. He wanted to preach simultaneously to the world by television, radio, video, and other media means. I think that his vision did not happen because he only reached one billion people. ONE BILLION PEOPLE by ONE MAN. Was that failure? I can just imagine that meeting when the idea was brought up for discussion:

"Do you know how much that would cost?"

"That is technically impossible!"

"We can't get that done!"

I can just hear Dr. Graham as he might have responded, "This is a God-sized vision; let us do it for His glory."

We live in a technologically advanced world. Now I know most of us still have VHS machines flashing 12:00. However, there are men and women who can make almost anything happen with today's opportunities.

God is simply looking for someone who will have an Acts 1:8 vision: a God Vision. Will you be one?

CHAPTER 2

EMPOWERED

"After that the Holy Spirit has come upon you,
then you shall be My witnesses,
first in Jerusalem, then in Judea, then Samaria,
and the uttermost parts of the world."

Acts 1:8 is likely one of the most widely known scriptures in the Church. Sadly, it is also probably one of the least practiced. We know we are to be witnesses of our faith in Christ, but we have successfully rationalized and excused ourselves from actually getting around to doing it. We keep careful records of our baptismal successes, but fail to note that we are losing the battle, even in the statistical work. According to the Southern Baptist Convention International Mission Board, for the first time ever, International Mission Board missionaries saw more than 500,000 people baptized. While we rejoice with each and every one of these, we must also let the reality penetrate our minds that there were probably 20 times that number born in the same year. We are reaching more people than ever before, but getting further behind because we simply are not getting the job done. Why? The answer is simple. We have only a few Christians who have ever led anyone to faith in Christ. Several have pointed out that only 5% of Christians will ever lead anyone to faith in Christ alone as Savior. That simply means that 95% of all professed Christians are failing to fulfill the Acts 1:8 vision. They may be personally saved but will do nothing to help anyone else ever make that decision. There is a real drought of power in the Church today because Mr. Average Christian is spiritually powerless!

Most Christians are literally scared to death when it comes to sharing their faith. They are afraid to offend someone by their sharing, while seemingly unaware that we are offending an Almighty God by our failure to share. We are more afraid of our peers than of our God. Christians are afraid someone might ask them something they cannot answer. Nowhere in the Bible does it say that we are to know everything. Only God knows everything!

I once heard a story of an alcoholic who had literally drunk the meaning out of his life. The car had been repossessed, the house was on the verge of being reclaimed by the bank, and his job was in jeopardy. His marriage was crumbling, and his children were afraid of him. He sought help and was wonderfully and miraculously saved by God's grace and mercy. He apologized to his wife and children, and went to his creditors to make things right. He took two weeks vacation from his work and began a diligent, intense study of the Bible. He knew he was going to have to face his drinking buddies at work and wanted to be ready. He, his wife, and pastor prayed earnestly that God would give Him words to say to his buddies to help them find Jesus. That fateful day arrived when he had to face his work friends. All morning he was greeted with sneers of "Hello, Preacher!" Break time came all too quickly for him, so with a prayer of "help" on his tongue, he moved into the break area. His taunting buddies surrounded him. "Hey, Preacher," they chided. "I understand you got religion and ain't drinking no more."

Hesitantly, he began his answer. "No, I did not get religion, but I gave my heart and life to Jesus Christ, as my Savior and Lord, and with His help I have been sober for two weeks."

"Well, Preacher," a buddy smiled. "I understand Jesus can turn water into wine." This caught the neophyte Christian by surprise, and he thought long and hard before he answered, "I don't really know about that yet; but if you will come over to my house I'll show you how Jesus changed wine and beer into furniture, and people into a family." Yes, he was empowered by the Holy Spirit even as a newborn Christian.

Christians are afraid someone might ridicule them if they are witnesses for Jesus. No one enjoys being ridiculed for any reason. Our standard human reaction to ridicule is flight or fight. (We run away or fight.) Neither of these two options is pleasant or acceptable for the Christian, so we just stay silent.

Jesus had a lifetime of ridicule from the religious world, but He was willing to endure it for God's sake. He taught us, "Blessed are you when men insult you and persecute you, and say all manner of evil against you falsely for my name's sake." (Matthew 5:11-12; key verse is 11.) Now it is, indeed, hard to get fired up about ridicule. However, Jesus said we will be blessed (happy) as a result of standing firm in the face of ridicule.

A couple of bullies approached a thin young man showing off his new Cadillac convertible. The larger of the two bullies grabbed the young man, pulled him out of the Cadillac, and drew a circle on the ground. He said menacingly, "You get out of that circle and I'll beat you to death." The two then proceeded to kick the new car. While they were demolishing the automobile, they would glance at the wimp in the circle. He was smiling, then grinning ear to ear, and then finally, laughing uncontrollably. This infuriated the bullies, prompting even more destruction of the automobile. Having devastated the new car, they rushed to the laughing wimp.

"Are you crazy?" they demanded. "We have destroyed your car and you are laughing uncontrollably." The man kept laughing.

"Tell us why you are laughing or we'll do the same to you!"

Finally, the young man stopped laughing long enough to say, "Well, while you two were destroying my car, I done stepped out of this circle three times, and you didn't even know it!"

God does not want us to be naive in the face of ridicule like the young man. But He does want to *empower* us to stand boldly before others.

Other Christians do not witness because they are either unconcerned or unmoved by the lostness of their friends and neighbors. Perhaps they truly do not believe in the reality of hell. However, the Bible is filled with scriptures attesting to hell's reality. The greatest Biblical proclaimer of the reality of hell was Jesus Christ Himself, as He constantly warned people to avoid hell at all costs (Matthew 5:22, 10:28) Because hell is real, we cannot be indifferent to the plight of our friends and neighbors.

Perhaps some Christians escape from the guilt of indifference by assuring themselves that someone else will reach the lost that they see in their paths each day. The hard truth is that, while we truly hope that this is so, the fact remains that people are dying by the thousands daily, without Jesus Christ. We must not shirk our duty to bear witness of Christ, because the price of failure is too high–an eternity in hell.

Some other Christians might just live so selfishly as to say by their lifestyle choices, "I'm saved and that is all that matters." This lifestyle of purposeful indifference to the lostness of others is the ultimate act of selfishness and by itself is ample evidence that the salvation in such a lifestyle is in doubt. Acts 1:8 says "...when the Holy Spirit has come upon you, you *shall* be my witnesses..." (NASB). A commitment to witnessing is not an option. Real Christians are empowered to witness and must practice their witness.

Other Christians might adopt the life philosophy that because God is good, He will not allow lost people to stay lost and go to hell. God in His goodness will provide a way for all to be saved.

The truth is that it is not God's will for any to perish in hell, but that all may be saved. (See 2 Peter 3:9.) God in His grace has provided a way for all men to be saved (See John 3:16-18), but when men reject or neglect so great a salvation that God has provided, there is no escape, and they will spend eternity in hell. (See Hebrews 2:3) No matter how hard we try to convince ourselves that our silence about our faith is of little consequence, the reality is that it is eternally significant. Romans 10: 8-15 (NASB) reads: "But what does it say? 'The word is near you, in your mouth and in your heart' — that is, the word of faith which we are preaching, that if you confess with your mouth Jesus as Lord, and believe in your heart that God raised Him from the dead, you will be saved; for with the heart person believes, resulting in righteousness, and with the mouth he confesses, resulting in salvation. For the scripture says, 'Whoever believes in Him will not be disappointed.' For there is no distinction between Jew and Greek; for the same Lord is Lord of all, abounding in riches for all who call on Him; for 'whoever will call on the name of the Lord will be saved.' How then will they call on Him in whom they have not believed? How will they believe in Him whom they have not heard? And how will they hear without a preacher? How will they preach unless they are sent? Just as it is written, 'How beautiful are the feet of those who bring good news of good things!'"

The reality is that we are losing the battle for the soul of mankind. The Church has settled, for the most part, for mediocrity. We have decided that comfort is more important than confrontation, and most Christians have adopted a non-Biblical worldview and a non-Biblical Jesus. Our drought of prayer is evident to people in the world. What, then, are we to do to regain the high ground of a Church On Mission? We must be empowered by the Holy Spirit and consent to follow His plan: The Acts 1:8 Strategy.

What is the Acts 1:8 Strategy?

It is the God-inspired vision of reaching our world with the Gospel message of Christ Jesus, one person at a time.

A good friend and I recently shared about the absence of real revival in the world. Here's a summary of our conversation:

We have lots of meetings that we call revivals, but real revival never takes place. Occasionally a few people will experience real revival and, mercifully, we experience a "drop of rain of revival" in a church, but in over 100 years there has been no sweeping revival in America. The evidence of real revival is not a stirring, but a real and permanent change in a person and a church.

In over thirty years of ministry, I have seen revival only three times. These experiences were awesome and unexplainable except that I saw what God did. Each time I was not really expecting revival, although I was praying for revival. God moved in and took over, and a church and people were permanently changed.

I had been asked to preach a revival meeting by our Home Mission Board in Glace Bay, Nova Scotia, Canada in 1981. Glace Bay is on the far northwestern tip of Nova Scotia and was a cold place, physically and spiritually. I flew there in October and was met at the airport by the pastor and his wife. We drove from Halifax to Glace Bay, and I had the opportunity to enjoy the natural beauty of Nova Scotia and to get to know the pastor. He and his wife were from Newfoundland. They were nice enough people but not full of the energy and personality of life. In fact, it seemed like it was going to be a long week. I discovered during the trip that they had done basically no preparation for revival and by their conversation, really had no expectations of anything significant happening. After arriving at the church home, I excused myself early that night to tuck myself into the white flannel sheets that felt warm against the cold Nova Scotia air. I spent a long time in prayer, making myself available to the Lord for anything He might want to do that week. I prayed for a change in me and a change in the pastor and the church. I fell asleep with little expectation about what God could or would do.

After breakfast the next morning we left the parsonage and walked across the driveway to the little white framed church. They had Sunday School for the children but nothing for adults. The 150 seat auditorium had about 50 people in attendance. The church was cold inside, with little heat, and with little spiritual power or desire. The singing service was right in line with the temperature and spiritual condition. I was introduced basically, "This is Dr. Michael Gravette. He has come from the United States to preach for us." I was hardly overwhelmed by the enthusiasm of the pastor or the congregation. I struggled in the message in trying to elicit some response from the crowd, to little avail. I opened the invitation more out of habit than conviction. There was one verse of invitation offered when the pastor abruptly stopped the invitation and closed the service.

A young red-headed woman, attractive and well-dressed, had moved to the first pew at the end of the first verse of the invitation. She was totally ignored by the pastor as he announced the end of the service and invited everyone back at 6:00 PM for "more of the same." He then went to the back of the church to "greet" the people who cleared the building in record time. The lady remained on the front pew. Finally, not knowing the customs in Glace Bay, I moved to her side and asked, "Are you a member of the church here?"

"No," she replied. "This is my first time."

"Why did you come forward today?" I questioned.

"I came to ask Jesus into my life." she responded.

Immediately I got excited. I motioned to the pastor who was waiting to leave with his wife, near the back door. I almost shouted, "This lady wants to receive Christ."

"Oh, well, get her name and we will talk to her later," came his unimpressed reply.

I could feel the hair on my neck standing up straight and the flush of my anger colored my neck and face. I excused myself and walked quickly to the pastor (much my elder) and in very demanding tones, said, "Get down here with me now!"

Shocked, he followed. I had the privilege of leading this sweet lady to Jesus as we knelt on the front pew. The pastor actually knelt with us in prayer. She asked us immediately, "Can you come to my house today and share Jesus with my husband?"

The pastor said, "Well, we'll come by sometime this week…"

I broke in quickly and said, "What time would you like us to come?"

She said, "Can you come about three?"

"Give your address to the pastor, and we will be there." I said. We all four then left the church.

We spoke little at lunch, only polite conversation among the three of us, but the pastor was ready to leave for the visit at 2:30. We arrived at the house which was obviously very upscale for Glace Bay and what I had seen of Nova Scotia thus far.

Jane greeted me at the door with a smile and a warm hug. She introduced me to her husband. He was over six feet tall and very professional and stoic in his demeanor. In our small talk I was told he owned three McDonald's franchises, was making more money than he could spend, and was quite content without church, thank you very much!

I told him I was not there to talk about church, but I did want to talk with him about Jesus and eternity. He looked startled, but allowed me to share. I told him the story of the rich young ruler (Matthew 19:16-26), and within a few minutes tears had begun to fill his eyes as I shared the greatest gift of all. He prayed to receive Christ. Even the pastor got happy! All the way back to the church, the pastor talked about how great that was and how long it had been since he had led someone to Christ.

We sat in the church, shared, and prayed for an hour until the service began. We walked into the church that had over 60 people there, including Jane and her husband, his parents, and their two boys. The singing was a little better, and the pastor was on a spiritual high. I preached, and Jane's whole family came forward as the pastor and I led them individually to Jesus. We set baptism for Monday night.

It was the first baptism in that church in over two years. That night few left the church after the service, and the pastor wanted to talk all night. I finally said, "I have got to go to bed!"

Monday morning was a morning of joy as the pastor continued his personal revival. I had never seen someone change so completely, so quickly! The church was packed the rest of the week as God showed up. It was awesome. People arrived an hour early each night, brought friends, and hugged, and talked, and sang. No one wanted to leave the church. The Morman missionaries in the area were saved. Jehovah's Witnesses came and gave their hearts to Jesus. I had never seen a church and a pastor change like this. Real revival had happened.

Saturday night over 200 people stood or sat, and watched the pastor on fire baptize 20 people. There was singing like I had never heard there before, and the service lasted past 10:00. We finally had to ask people to leave. Real life-changing revival had come to Glace Bay that week, and it remained in changed lives. God did something wonderful. He in His sovereignty showed up despite me, the pastor, and the church. Why? Mercy? Grace?

Love? Since Glace Bay, I have only seen it duplicated twice -- once the next year in Sydney, Nova Scotia, and once in Dothan, Alabama. Why? I do not know. Revival is a sovereign work of God. When He moves us it is awesome, but we cannot duplicate revival. What can we do then?

We must first adopt God's worldview as expressed in the Bible. Before we can do that, however, we must adopt a higher view of God. He is God, and we are not. Life is about God and our desire to have a personal relationship with Him through Jesus Christ. We cannot change or manipulate God. He is Almighty and His will *will* be done. He will send revival as He pleases, and He will withhold it as He pleases. However, we can and must claim His promises and stand on those promises. I have seen real revival three times. Try as I have, I have not been able to duplicate them. So why plan, claim promises, and do meetings?

God shows up in many ways. There are usually a few people who experience real revival in their lives. It might not be church wide, but God still touches individual lives with His power.

God's worldview is to reach the world, one person at a time. There is no wasted effort when the seed is sown. We are to be sowers of the seed, knowing that God alone brings the harvest. Our planning, praying, and claiming, allows us to be successful sowers of the word. We are successful when we share, preach, and pray. That is our part. God's part is the harvest.

Even though I have seen only three real churchwide revivals, I have seen thousands of individuals revived. I have had my own life revived dozens of times. God has shown up in my life time and time again, and empowered me to keep on moving. He has revived me and thousands of others who keep on faithfully sowing the Gospel.

God's worldview places the Biblical Christ at the center of His plan. Jesus said, "And I, if I am lifted up from the earth, will draw all men to myself" (John 12:32, NASB). God has chosen to give Jesus the name above every name, and place Him at the epicenter of all His creation on earth and in heaven.

All of our strategic planning must be centered around the Biblical worldview that all life is about Jesus Christ and finding our place in Him. This concept should dominate our planning and strategy.

Another concept in the Biblical worldview is that the Bible is the Word of God. It contains the way of salvation, hope, and right relationship between God and man. In the Bible we will find the answers we are looking for and a firm foundation on which to build our lives, families, and futures.

An important Biblical worldview that will shape our lives is that God's desire is for all to be saved. Now if this is true, it is evident that Acts 1:8 has great authority. It demonstrates that we must find a way to reach the man next door as well as those in the next town, our state, and all countries. God loves each person and assigns eternal values to the soul of that individual. We must, therefore, intentionally find a way to get the Gospel to every person. No one can be viewed as outside the love and will of God. No one is considered below us or above us, as we seek out God's plan for their lives.

If we adopt God's Biblical worldview, it, by definition, will change our reality, shape our goals, and render important every hour and every day. As we realize that each person we meet or pass is important to God, that person becomes important to us, so they are objects of our planning and intentional efforts.

The Biblical worldview also sets the standard by which we are to live. Right or wrong is not an individual preference, a majority vote, or even some mystic standardized cultural behavior. Rather, it is the rock solid command of an almighty and omnipotent God. It is God who calls right "righteousness" and wrong "sin." When our behavior differs from that described in the Bible, it is our behavior that is wrong and must be corrected. When God says, "Ye shall be my witnesses," He means each born-again believer is to witness our faith and relationship to Him in Jesus. Failure to be a witness is opposed to God's will and therefore declared as sin against God. When we adopt the Biblical world view of Acts 1:8, it requires us to set a strategy to reach everyone, no exceptions, one person at a time.

How will we reach the world? For the natural man it is impossible, and so that has never been the intent of God. We must be changed by the Holy Spirit of God. He is able to give us new eyes and a new heart. When the Holy Spirit changes our lives we become empowered individuals.

The New Testament Christian often marked the conversion of a new disciple by adopting a name change. This, of course, had massive Old Testament support when God changed Abram's name to Abraham, Sarai to Sarah, and Jacob's to Israel. Jesus changed Levi to Matthew, Simon to Peter, and Saul to Paul. So marked was the change of nature by the Holy Spirit in these believers that they had to celebrate this difference by name changes.

Now a name change has no real meaning if it is not accompanied by a change in nature by the Holy Spirit. Paul described it thus:

Galatians 2:20–"I have been crucified with Christ; and it is no longer I who live, but Christ lives in me; and the life which I now live in the flesh I live by faith in the Son of God, who loved me, and gave Himself up for me."

Philippians 1:21–"For me to live is Christ, and to die is gain."

2 Corinthians 5:17–"Therefore if anyone is in Christ, he is a new creature; the old things passed away; behold, new things have come."

An Acts 1:8 strategy will be effective only to the extent we allow the Holy Spirit to make a difference in our lives and the way we "see" our world and our neighbor. The Holy Spirit wants every man to be our neighbor and teaches us that every man is worthy of our full efforts.

Jesus defined the Biblical worldview of a neighbor in the Parable of the Good Samaritan (Luke 10:30-37):

"Jesus replied and said, 'A man was going down from Jerusalem to Jericho, and fell among robbers, and they stripped him and beat him, and went away leaving him half dead. And by chance a priest was going down on that road, and when he saw him, he passed by on the other side. Likewise a Levite also, when he came to the place and saw him, passed by on the other side. But a Samaritan, who was on a journey, came upon him; and when he saw him, he felt compassion, and came to him, and bandaged up his wounds, pouring oil and wine on them; and he put him on his own beast, and brought him to an inn and took care of him. On the next day he took out two denarii and gave them to the innkeeper and said, 'Take care of him; and whatever more you spend, when I return I will repay you.' Which of these three do you think proved to be a neighbor to the man who fell into the robbers' hands?' And he said, 'The one who showed mercy toward him.' And Jesus said to him, 'Go and do the same.'"

To reach our neighbor we must allow the Holy Spirit to change us to be spiritual fruit bearers. The Holy Spirit is in the fruit-bearing business. He will provide both internal and external fruit to the truly submitted disciple.

Each disciple needs to bear internal fruit (Rom. 5:3-4; II Cor. 6:6; 8:7). This fruit is commonly known as the fruit of the Spirit, found listed in Galatians 5:22-23: "But the fruit of the Spirit is love, joy, peace, patience, kindness, goodness, faithfulness, gentleness, self-control." These are fruit that the Holy Spirit produces in the life of every believer. This internal fruit is produced in the disciple as he tries to be an imitator of Christ (I Peter 2:21). As the disciple imitates Jesus, the Holy Spirit will produce Jesus-like fruit. The disciple who lives as Jesus cannot help but produce a fruit similar to the fruit Jesus produced. We must imitate Jesus.

While relaxing at home one evening, the children were playing and watching television. Michael, Jr., who was five, would put his feet up on the arm of the chair to watch television. Tara, the two-year-old, would do the exact same thing in her chair. Michael would get a pillow, Tara would get a pillow. Tara was imitating every little action of her big brother. The disciple who imitates every action of Jesus will soon experience the fruitfulness of the Holy Spirit in his life. Jesus said the disciple is to "be perfect" as God in heaven is perfect (Matt. 5:48). The fruit of the Holy Spirit is perfection in the same manner as God is perfect. This is the internal work of the Holy Spirit. The Holy Spirit works from the inside out in the life of the believer. As the disciple dies to himself (John 12:24; Eph. 4:22), the Holy Spirit can do more of His internal work. The transforming power of the Holy Spirit is continually making the disciple a new creation. This activity is completed only when the inside transformation takes charge of the outside as well. As the disciple is turned inside out, he can produce external fruit, too.

The disciple is to bear external fruit. Matthew 28:19 asserts that a disciple is to be the product of another disciple. A disciple is the external fruit of another disciple. Often this miracle of reproduction comes slowly to a new disciple. The disciple is not to be discouraged by lack of results; rather, he is to sow the seed of salvation wherever he goes (Matt. 13:3). As mentioned earlier, the disciple is not responsible for the results, for that is God's responsibility; but the disciple is responsible for the sowing of salvation's seed.

To summarize then, the disciple is to bear internal and external fruit. Internal fruit is the direct result of the Holy Spirit producing His fruit in the disciple. Once this transformation takes place, the disciple can bear external fruit. External fruit is the sowing of the seed of salvation which will result in another disciple. These fruit are required of every follower of Jesus.

How can a disciple bear good spiritual fruit for God? It is thoroughly impossible for any Christian to produce good spiritual fruit. (If that is a surprise, reread the epistle to the Romans.) Spiritual fruit is the result of the Holy Spirit working in and through a disciple. The disciple can and must learn how to make himself more useable for the Holy Spirit.

The disciple must learn from God how to bear spiritual fruit. "If any of you lacks wisdom, let him ask of God who gives to all men generously and without reproach" (Jas. 1:5). God is eager to provide every disciple with wisdom necessary to be a "fertile field" for the Holy Spirit. Today, if one were to poll the successful farmers in the United States, he would probably discover that most are second, third, fourth, or more generation farmers. They have learned the land and good farming practices from their fathers and grandfathers. Their success is the result of accumulated knowledge over the years. Likewise, God is the source of all spiritual wisdom. He knows exactly what He wants and how to get it. God earnestly wants every disciple to be a successful fruit bearer. The disciple who goes to God and asks Him for wisdom is the disciple who has learned the secret to success. God's success is inseparable from Jesus.

The disciple must be in contact with Jesus to bear good fruit (John 15:4, Ps. 1;3, Matt. 13:23). If a person makes contact with electricity, it means he has plugged in to the source of the electrical power. Jesus is the source of the disciple's power to bear fruit. To plug into Jesus is to plug into the power of Almighty God. The disciple who is in contact with Jesus can do anything. He can produce the fruit of Jesus Christ Himself.

The disciple must learn to sow with patience (Heb. 10:36; Jas. 1:4; 5:7, Gal. 6:9). Patience is itself a fruit of the Spirit (Gal. 5:22-23). This fruit is one of the great virtues of a disciple. The disciple must learn to wait on God. God's time and man's time are not the same. Everyone has heard the stories of wives, husbands, mothers, or fathers praying for years for the salvation of that special family member. The question of why it takes so long will go unanswered until the heavenly kingdom comes; but the most important thing for a disciple to learn is not the why of things, but patience. God does not always include the disciple in all His time schedule planning. It is, therefore, absolutely necessary for the disciple to learn patience. Jesus Christ came to earth to die on the cross, but it took 33 years before that mission was accomplished. God promised Abraham a son. This son was the covenant son; yet it took many years before Isaac was born. Abraham needed patience because God knew the right time to send Isaac, just as He knew the right time for Jesus to die on the cross. The disciple must always be aware that God's time is the right time. It is important for the disciple to learn patience in his fruit bearing so that he can be on God's time schedule.

The disciple must learn that not every seed sown will produce fruit (Luke 8:5). The disciple is responsible only for the sowing of seeds (I Cor: 3:6-8), but God is responsible for the increase.

The disciple must learn that fruit bearing often involves teamwork (I Cor 3:6-9). God often carries out His plan through the work of many disciples. Very seldom does a person come forward in a worship service as the result of just the preaching. Usually his decision is the result of visits, family prayers, and witnessing teams. This is the type of teamwork God often uses. Simon Peter was brought to Jesus by his brother, Andrew. Paul was influenced by Stephen's death as a martyr, the dedication of many Christians he persecuted, and his Damascus Road experience. The disciple may never see the result of his work, but the seeds he sows might be part of the spiritual fruit of another disciple.

God always provides spiritual increase from spiritual seeds. The disciple must always sow spiritual seeds in order to bear spiritual fruit (Gal. 6:8). God is only interested in spiritual fruit. God has a law of nature called the "Law of Like Kind." This law, very simply stated, is that whatever seed you sow will produce fruit of the same kind. Apple seeds produce apples, corn seeds produce corn, and tomato seeds produce tomatoes. The disciple who wants to grow spiritual fruit must plant spiritual seed. Spiritual seed includes the Word of God, a testimony of Jesus Christ, a spiritual tract, and other spiritual sharing. These seeds can be sown by preaching, teaching, giving one's testimony, talking about the Lord, prayers and a lifestyle that reflects the Gospel. These are the types of seed that God will use to produce spiritual fruit. And the time that God wants the disciple to plant spiritual seeds is NOW!

The disciple must recognize that harvest time is now (John 4:35; Mark 4:29; Matt. 9:37). The time is past when a disciple can put off until tomorrow what must be done today. The time of Jesus' return is close at hand, and there are so many people in this world who need the Lord. Jesus has said that "the fields are ripe unto harvest, but the laborers are few" (John 4). This fact is very sad, but very true. The disciple has been given "now." Now is all anyone can be sure of. The disciple must be about the work of discipling now. Peanut farmers in Oklahoma plant and tend their crops at a somewhat leisurely pace. The rows and rows of peanuts are worked daily, but with little pressure on the farmer. Then comes the harvest, and the pace is suddenly quickened. Farmers from neighboring farms work together to get the harvest in before the peanuts rot on the vine. There is only so much time to harvest. A change in the weather, breakdown in machinery, or an illness can cause complete disaster. The peanut farmers will work day and night until the harvest is completed. Disciples must learn the urgency of their task. The harvest is ripe, so the time is short. The disciple must work daily with a sense of commitment so that not even one soul will be lost. Truly, the harvest is now. Oh, how sad that the laborers are so few! To those disciples who work continually in the harvest come rewards beyond their highest expectations.

How will spiritual fruit help the disciple? Spiritual fruit is proof of a maturing spiritual life. Many teenage boys check their height and weight, eagerly looking for a sign of growth. Many times middle-aged men and women check their weight hoping they have not grown! People are always looking for signs of growth in their own lives and the lives of those about them. The Christian is not an exception. The Christian looks for signs to see if he is maturing in the faith. Spiritual fruit provides an accurate measurement of one's growth in the Lord. As one experiences love, joy, peace, patience, and other internal fruit, he will know he is on the move spiritually. As the disciple sees a new disciple born as part of his labors, he can rejoice in his own growth. Spiritual fruit, whether external or internal, will help the disciple be aware of his growth or lack of growth. The fruitless Christian will be convicted, but the fruitful disciple will rejoice.

Spiritual fruit bearing allows the Holy Spirit free use of the disciple's life. A goal for every disciple is to be Spirit-filled and Spirit-controlled. The disciple who is producing much fruit is the disciple who is allowing the Spirit to control his life; thus, the Spirit is free to produce even more fruit. This cycle will become an upward spiral of good fruit bearing, as the disciple yields more of his life to the Holy Spirit. This type of spiritual fruit is eternal.

Spiritual fruit is eternal fruit. Spiritual fruit never spoils and is never used up. Spiritual fruit will follow the disciple to God's heavenly kingdom. This fruit will become part of the rewards for each faithful disciple. It will also provide a great joy as the disciple produces this fruit on earth.

Spiritual fruit is a source of joy to each disciple. Another fruit of the Spirit is joy. This joy is present in the life of a disciple as he labors and is heightened as he observes his labors.

There is a deep sense of fulfillment to the fruit bearing disciple. There is a deep sense of calmness, even in the storm. There was a farm couple who had been looking for a new worker to help on the farm. They had looked everywhere but had been unable to locate a good, dependable man. One morning as they were eating breakfast, there was a knock at the door. It was a stranger looking for a job. The farmer asked for his references, but the stranger simply said, "I can sleep when it storms." The farmer needed the help so much that he decided to take a chance on the stranger. He showed him all around the farm and pointed out the necessary chores. The farmer went about his daily routine and hardly saw the stranger. Finally, night fell, and the farmer and his wife went to sleep. The farmer was awakened about 2:00 AM by a severe storm. He quickly dressed and ran to the barn where he found the "hand" fast asleep. The farmer attempted twice, unsuccessfully, to awaken his "hand." He then left to check the farm all alone. He checked the corn bed, and it was safely covered and protected. He checked the wheat silo, and it, too, was protected. He checked the animals and found all safe, dry, and fed. He ran back to the house, having found everything as it should be. Then, and only then did he realize what the stranger meant when he said, "I can sleep when it storms."

The disciple must likewise be so prepared that he can sleep undisturbed. The harvest is ripe and the laborers are few. God wants disciples who can sleep in the storm. These disciples become the teachers of other disciples.

As we bear fruit we will have our vision to reach the world for Jesus elevated and clarified.

"Ye"–every Christian

"shall be"–command, not an option

"witnesses"–We are all witnesses good or bad. Someone is looking at your faith today. What will they see in you and hear from you? Amen

The Gospel According to You

The most beautiful story given to man
Was written long ago
By Matthew, Mark, Luke and John
Of Christ and His mission below.
And you write a gospel, a chapter a day,
By your deeds, whether faithless or true;
When others read it, what will they think
In the gospel according to you?
It's a wonderful story, the Gospel of love,
As it shines with Christ's life divine.
Oh that its truth might be told again
In the story of your life and mine.
You are writing each day a letter to all.
Take care that the writing is true.
It's the only gospel some people may read,
The gospel according to you.
Author unknown.

CHAPTER 3

EMPOWERED!
A NEW PERSPECTIVE

What does a new perspective have to do with anything? Everything! Can we not obtain a new perspective by just adopting God's Biblical worldview? Such a worldview allows us to see things as God sees them, and this new perspective allows us to see how God's vision, God's plan, and God's people come together to make things happen.

A new perspective allows us to function in a new paradigm. When we come to a sudden dead end, we develop a heretofore unknown perspective. When we see the world through God's eyes, and we are empowered by the Holy Spirit, we move into a plane we have not experienced before.

Elisha the prophet and his servant were spending the night in Dothan (II Kings 6:15-17). The servant awoke early and went for a walk to check the city out. He discovered that the city was totally surrounded by the enemy, seeking to kill Elisha. He rushed back to Elisha and told him the terrible news, but to his surprise, the prophet of God responded, "There are more of us than there are of them." Startled, the servant may have returned to the walls to count again. "Let's see, Elisha and me, that's two; and the enemy, one-two-three hundred or four hundred." He would then have returned to the prophet to advise him that his math was, indeed, correct, and Elisha had better do something–quick! The prophet prayed, "God, open his eyes." The servant went to the walls again to see the hills and heavens full of heavenly warriors, ready to fight for Elisha. His reaction (I paraphrase): "Yahoo! We have these guys just where we want them!"

What happened? There was the same reality, but with a different perspective! Does perspective change our outlook? Yes it does! It makes all the difference in the world. Instead of doing the same old stuff the same old way, ask God to open your eyes and give you a new perspective.

Over the past few years the prayer of Jabez has become a preferred prayer of many Christians. Jabez prayed that God would enlarge his tent. In my opinion, Jabez was asking God to give him a new perspective. We know that the "foolishness of God is wiser than men, and the weakness of God is stronger than men" (I Cor. 1:25). So if we are going to do what is impossible for man, we must actively seek out the perspective in which God issues His command. God would not ask us to reach for something that together we could not achieve. That would be ridiculous and self-defeating.

Winning our city, our state, our nation, and our world is one of those things that we can talk about, but we know that we will not accomplish. Why would God command us to walk an Acts 1:8 lifestyle if we all know it cannot be done?

Perhaps it is because our perspective is wrong. How does God see us and the world, and the challenge of Acts 1:8?

God sees us as *what we can be* when absolutely sold out to Him. Levi was a tax collector. He was a Jew who sold out to the Romans for money. The Romans did not like him because he was a Jew and just greedy. The Jews despised him because he took their money and got rich in the process. Levi had to "hang out" with other publicans (tax collectors) because few others would have anything to do with him. However, when Jesus met Levi, Jesus renamed him "Matthew," which means "Gift from God. The world saw Levi as trash. God saw him as treasure. That is a different perspective, indeed!

"Simon" means "little stone, or pebble." Simon was a brash, loud-mouthed fisherman who was impulsive, unstable, and aggressive. Jesus looked at Simon and said, "You are now Peter (the Rock), and upon this rock I will build My church." (Matthew 16:18; also see John 1:42.) God obviously saw something in Peter no one else did. God had a different perspective.

John was young, inexperienced, easily angered, and hard to control. He and his brother, James, were called "The Sons of Thunder." Yet, Jesus loved him so much that in his ministry years John earned the title "Apostle of Love." What a change! God, however, was not surprised because He had chosen John with all of his rough edges, proving His real potential. God had a different perspective. God not only sees people differently, He sees events and obstacles with a different perspective.

There they were, looking down on the wall of Jericho like it was an invincible, unscalable mountain. "What was a guy to do?" Joshua may have wondered. In man's eyes, "It cannot be done, no way, no how, no, no!" That would have been the unanimous vote of the entire Israeli army as they stood at a distance and just stared.

Then came God! "I want you to walk around the city one time for six days in absolute silence. Then on the seventh day I want you to walk around the city six times in silence. Then walk around the seventh time, and at the signal, blow your trumpet and shout to the top of your capacity!" A terrible plan from Israel's perspective, but God had a differing one. Israel reluctantly did it God's way, and you know the rest of the story: The walls fell and Jericho was captured!

There they were in a field a long way away from everything! Five thousand men, plus. They were hungry, tired, and ready to eat. They had been blessed by the teaching of Jesus, but now their physical need seemed to overwhelm their spiritual need. Andrew had a little boy bring him his lunch of five small loaves and two small fish, and Andrew did what Andrew always did (John 6:8-9). He took him to Jesus.

He said, "Lord, there is a lad here with a small lunch, but what is this among so many?" Andrew shared the perspective of everyone there. Jesus saw the lad, the lunch, and Andrew, and said, "Have the people sit down, spread their picnic cloths, get out their forks and get ready to eat." (My translation)

Why? He saw things differently. All the people were filled. No more hunger.

I could give dozens of other examples, but perhaps you will agree with me now that God often sees things differently than man sees things.

Business as usual tells us that it is impossible and cannot be done. Satan whispers in our ear, "Don't go there, it is not worth the failure."

Business as usual says, "Just do the best you can, and we can always say we tried."

Business as usual says, "Be comfortable, be safe, trust your own instincts and wisdom!"

God says, "Trust me." (Proverbs 3:5-6) "Acknowledge me and obey me." How can we acknowledge God?

First, just let God be God! He is a nothing-is-impossible God! When Jesus gave the disciples Acts 1:8, He gave it to them so that they would get it done. It was given not as a goal, but as a mission. He gave it to the church as a plan to be detailed, not as something to sit around and wish or dream about.

Second, we must acknowledge God by taking Him at His Word. If He says it can be done, it can be done. That's called believing.

Peter again: This time he and the group had been fishing all night. They had cleaned their nets and were ready to go home to sleep. Then Jesus commandeered his fishing boat for a pulpit (Luke 5:1-11). After Jesus had finished his message, He said, "Peter, go back to the deep water and put out your nets for a catch."

That was the last thing Peter wanted to hear. "But Lord, we have fished all night and caught nothing; but at your word, we will do it!" It made no sense to Peter. He was too tired anyway. He wanted to go home, but he believed Jesus, and obeyed. They caught so many fish the nets broke! Peter obeyed God, trusted God's perspective, and was blessed beyond measure. We acknowledge God when we obey Him, despite our perspective. This is the root of faith.

"Now faith is the substance of things hoped for, the evidence of things not seen. For by it the elders obtained a good report. Through faith we understand that the worlds were framed by the word of God, so that things which are seen were not made of things which do appear. By faith Abel offered unto God a more excellent sacrifice than Cain, by which he obtained witness that he was righteous, God testifying of his gifts: and by it he being dead yet speaketh.

"By faith Enoch was translated that he should not see death; and was not found, because God had translated him: for before his translation he had this testimony, that he pleased God. But without faith it is impossible to please him: for he that cometh to God must believe that he is, and that he is a rewarder of them that diligently seek him.

By faith Noah, being warned of God of things not seen as yet, moved with fear, prepared an ark to the saving of his house; by the which he condemned the world, and became heir of the righteousness which is by faith." (Hebrews 11:1-17 KJV)

These people all followed God's perspective by faith, and it changed their lives. Obedience to His commands is essential to getting the impossible accomplished.

How do we get this new perspective to make things happen?

1. Ask God to open our eyes to see what He sees.
2. Ask God for the desire to walk by faith.
3. Claim God's word (Acts 1:8) as true.
4. Build your plans to do it.
5. Present those plans to God and ask Him to change anything, or everything!
6. Commit to the plan.
7. Watch God work.

Jesus came to earth as a baby born of a virgin and led a perfect sin-free life that was absolutely pleasing to God. He prayed daily for God to open His eyes so that He could see God's perspective. He walked in the wilderness, with Satan shadowing Him at every step, asking God to give Him the will to do it God's way. Satan offered "better" plans, but Jesus claimed God's Word as true and claimed God's plan. "Man shall not live on bread alone, but on every word that proceeds out of the mouth of God." (Matthew 4:4)

Jesus then organized a plan to accomplish the mission. He called 12 disciples to train and leave behind, and "set his face like flint toward Jerusalem." He presented his plans to God and gave God permission to change anything, but God responded, "This is My beloved Son, in whom I am well pleased." (Matthew 3:17) Jesus then committed to the plan and obeyed. "Not my will, but Yours be done." (Luke 22:42) Then He was nailed to a cross and died.

What went wrong? He failed! He was defeated! Satan has won! What do we do now? "My God, my God, why have you forsaken me?" (Matthew 27:46; Psalm 22:1)

Every disciple, Mary his mother, and all the followers saw the cross and cried, "Defeat! Defeat! Defeat!"

However, God saw the cross and cried, "It is finished!" Completed! Victory! He stamped it so in just three days on Resurrection Sunday!

Acts 1:8 is the plan. Get the perspective, and get on with it.

What do you need to do to start an Acts 1:8 life and church? Simply put, the will to do it. It has to start somewhere with someone. Put self and fear aside and dive into the work with God's power and your personal testimony.

For several years my wife and I had gone on January Bible cruises in the Carribean. They were some wonderful times, listening to great preachers like Adrian Rogers, Jerry Vines, Jim Henry, and Johnny Hunt. Also, sharing on these cruises as my favorite gospel group, "Greater Vision." "Greater Vision" is a trio which includes Rodney Griffin, one of the truly great Gospel song writers alive today. Rodney was in a Bible study on the cruise with Adrian Rogers, who was preaching on the man who was brought to Jesus by His four friends, and the friends tore open the roof of a house to get their friend to Jesus. (Mark 2:1-12)

Adrian Rogers then went on to illustrate what those four friends might have said as they brought their friend to Jesus. Rodney Griffin then took this illustration and wrote my favorite Gospel song. Here are the words:

My Name Is Lazarus

One day four men brought a crippled man to Jesus
Still and lifeless, he lay upon his bed
He had not moved since he was just a baby
Still he longed to become a normal man.

Now we don't know much about the men that carried
The corners of his tattered bed that day
But if we may create an illustration
We'll see what these men might have had to say

Suppose that first man said, "I hate to doubt it
For Jesus touched my eyes when I was blind
He made me see and there's no doubt about it
But this man's needs are more serious than mine"

Suppose that second man said, "No need to bother
This man's condition will remain the same
Though Jesus touched my hand when it was withered
I don't believe he can heal a man so lame"

Suppose that third man said, "I hate to question
But no one here is more skeptical than me.
Though Jesus cleansed me when I was a leper
This helpless man will never walk you see."

Then every eye was turned to the fourth man
To see how he might criticize and doubt
But all three men were startled with amazement
When that fourth man stopped and said his name out loud.

CHORUS

He said "My name is Lazarus, could I testify?
My name is Lazarus, feels good to be alive!

When I in chains of death was bound
This man named Jesus called me out!
If you think your little problem is too big for Him to solve,
Take it from the one who's heard the mighty voice of God
A living testimony of His death-defying touch
My name is LAZARUS! (Used by Permission)

Now Lazarus had a testimony and the will to share it at any cost. Do you have a testimony about who God is; what Jesus did; and how it has changed you life? That's all you need to get started if you add the will to step out on the Acts 1:8 mission and promise.

If we accept Acts 1:8 as the passionate heart of God, then we must evaluate our desire to center our will to His will. If we can honestly say that we have the desire to get "On Mission with God," it is then time to make the commitment.

Years ago I pastored in Florala, Alabama. We lived with our small children next to the church in a beautiful old two-story pastorium. The house had 14-foot high ceilings with a beautiful staircase leading to the second floor. I used this staircase to promote an illustration between genuine commitment and merely talking a good game. If I had placed my two-year-old daughter up on the top of those stairs and said "Jump to Daddy," she would have jumped with little hesitation because she trusted her daddy and knew I would not allow her to be hurt. If I had put my five-year-old son on that staircase and said, "Jump to Daddy, son," he would have said,

"Will you catch me, Daddy?"

"Yes, son."

"Do you promise you will catch me, Daddy?"

"Yes, son, I promise."

Then he would have reluctantly jumped. He wanted to jump but he just needed some encouragement. If I put my wife up there and said "Jump, Baby," she would walk away and say, "Don't be silly!"

Did that mean that she did not love me or trust me? No. She loves and trusts me, but she would not jump. All her will says,

"Protect yourself!" Experience says that it cannot be done. Physics says that someone will be hurt. Humanly speaking, it would be very difficult, even though my wife would have trusted me to catch my children. It is hard to put our humanity, our experience, our wisdom, our understanding aside and say, "I'll jump to God even if it can't be done."

Don't be afraid to lead the way.

CHAPTER 4

THE POWER TO
GET THINGS DONE

Nike's commercial marketing slogan is "Just do it." This has been a successful tool for them, and I need to borrow it to say, "God says, 'Just do it.'" God has provided the power we need to get the Acts 1:8 strategy accomplished.

Trust in the Lord with all your heart
And do not lean on your own understanding.
In all your ways acknowledge Him,
And He will make your paths straight.
- Proverbs 3:5-6

Believe me, I know somewhat of how gigantic this mission is, but I also keep reminding myself of the size of my God and the power He has.

Almighty God, or "El Shaddai" is one of my favorite names that the Bible uses to describe God. "All" means just that: ALL! He is fully "mighty." He has and controls all the might and power there is. He does not just have more power than anyone in the universe; rather, He *is* the seat of all power.

Jesus put it this way in Matthew 28:18, "All power (author-ity) is given unto me in heaven and in earth" (KJV). Again, there is that little all-inclusive word, "all." God has placed in the hands of Jesus Christ, King of Kings, and Lord of Lords, all the power there is in the universe. He says he has all power "in heaven and in earth." Biblically, that simply means "everywhere." There is not a niche in the universe that has power that is not in God's hands. Even Satan and all (inclusive) his demons have what power they have by God's permission. Satan and his demons know their ultimate fate, and they know that they can do nothing to alter their fate.

Mark 5:1-14 tells the story of the Gerasene demoniac from whom Jesus sent several hundreds of demons into swine. They had begged Jesus not to send them to the "pit," their ultimate destiny.

James 2:19 states, "You believe that God is one. You do well; the demons also believe, and shudder." Satan and his demons exercise their power only within the constraints that God places upon them, which He can, and has revoked at His pleasure.

What power does God have? It is God's own power! It is the power that God used to create the world and all there is in it. This is the power that God has by His nature! His power can speak life and planets into existence. His power is omniscient (all knowing) and omnipresent. There is no secret that is kept from Him and no place to hide where He cannot see and know us. His power is transparent, so that all might see it and be amazed by it. His power can stop the earth from rotating (Joshua 10:13). God's power came upon a virgin and she conceived a boy child named Jesus (Matthew 1:18).

God parted the Red Sea and allowed the Israelites to cross over on dry land (Exodus 14:21). Jesus raised Lazarus from the dead (John 11). Jesus calmed the storm and controlled the weather (Matthew 8:26). These are but a small handful of occasions when God has shown His power. However, Jesus told his disciples of an upcoming event that would empower His followers to do the "same" works. This event would be the coming of the Holy Spirit to dwell permanently in the life of each believer (John 14:1-21).

The Holy Spirit of God is the energy or the power of God. At Pentecost the Holy Spirit came upon the believers and remained on them (Acts 2:1-4). These believers then became walking power instruments as they served the Holy Spirit of Almighty God. The disciples did the impossible again and again. Miracles became an accepted way of life. People in Ephesus even took handkerchiefs from Paul and laid them on the ill, and they were healed. (Acts 19:11-20)

The greatest miracle was that they all became witnesses of Jesus Christ with power to turn the world up- side down. This is the power that God has for each of us who will take the Acts 1:8 command seriously. There is no task too great and no obstacle too large that a Holy Spirit inspired Christian and church cannot overcome.

Where does this power come from? It comes from God through Jesus Christ by the Holy Spirit to every born again Christian. This means You. The power is already in you ready to make you a God-anointed empowered soldier of Jesus Christ (Ephesians 6:12-20).

To receive the power of the Holy Spirit within us is to have the full capacity of God at our disposal. When you combine Holy Spirit power with an Acts 1:8 desire, the resulting plan has the potential to affect eternity.

How do we get this combination activated in our lives and our churches?

One, claim it as a God honoring promise. God's promises are often contingent upon our claiming them. God has commanded us to be witnesses to our Jerusalem and the uttermost parts of the world, and has provided the Holy Spirit as our guide and power. It stands to reason that He will move mountains to get us on the move and to accomplish this vision. It is left up to us to claim His promise and plug into the power He has provided.

Years ago, when Elvis Presley was alive, it is said that he would slip out of Graceland and visit the local Cadillac dealership. Many times he would buy a new Cadillac for a total stranger. Suppose you were one of those unknowing car shoppers (possibly just wishing, not knowing you could own a Cadillac for your own!). Suddenly, a salesman approaches you and says that Elvis Presley has just purchased a Cadillac for you—just come into the office and sign the papers. Perhaps you might have said, "Oh sure, Elvis is buying me a car," and gone home. The car was yours; all you had to do was claim it, but if you failed to claim it for whatever reason, you lost the opportunity!

A man had a dream that he had died and gone to heaven. It was, of course, even more beautiful and wonderful than he had ever imagined. He stood there in awe, not knowing what to do next. An angel approached him and said, "I am your guide to show you around heaven." They went everywhere. First to the throne of God and at His right hand, Jesus. The man laid all his crowns at Jesus' feet and worshiped Him. Next they visited his mansion, the streets of gold, the gates of pearl. As they walked back and forth across heaven, the angel pointed out everything and explained in detail every site and every street, and answered every question.

The man had noticed a large warehouse that the angel had pointedly ignored each time they passed it. After the third time the man questioned the angel, "What is this warehouse?"

The angel kindly responded, "You do not want to know."

"Yes, the man persisted, "I want to know everything about heaven."

The angel moved to the multistory warehouse and opened the huge door. Inside the man saw boxes stacked from the floor to the ceiling. The warehouse was literally packed with only a few dozen boxes missing. The angel said quietly, "These are the blessings God wanted to give you that you left unclaimed."

Claim your blessing of God's power in your life.

Next, find where God is working and join in what He is doing. Henry Blackaby and others have correctly noted that God is always up to something. Find out where He is showing up, and get there as quickly as you can.

God is showing up in different kinds of places these days. If you would take the Spanish version of the "Jesus" film with you to the Yucatan Peninsula in Mexico, and show it every night, moving from place to place, you could see dozens, if not hundreds of people come to see this film and receive Christ as Savior. I believe we could start a church every night in Cancun if we had enough trained Mexican leaders in place. God is working there. God is working through the "The Passion of the Christ" by Mel Gibson. It is truly amazing to see millions of people flocking to see this movie and being moved in new ways. They come out seeking more about this Jesus.

God is working in Moldova, in China, in unprecedented ways. He just needs "witnesses" to come and join Him in what He is doing.

Third, be willing to adjust your plan to His plan. The power falls where God sends it. We must work our plan to match God's plan. Simon, the magician in Acts 8:9-24, thought he could buy the power of God. Judas Iscariot thought he could manipulate the power of God. The disciples in the valley thought they could take a shortcut to get to God's power (Matthew 17:14-23) but they failed. They had their own agenda, not God's agenda. Our plan must match God's plan.

Pray, seeking God's will, and plan for the life of your church, and your own life! Prayer is meant to be a powerful weapon in our spiritual arsenal. However, it is my observation that prayer is one of the most neglected weapons in our churches. Oh yes, we pray, but for the most part our prayers really do not change anything.

One of my favorite stories in the Bible is found in Acts 12:3-16. Peter had been thrown into jail for bearing witness for Jesus. The church had gathered to pray him out of jail. God heard their prayers and miraculously freed Peter from jail. Peter knew exactly where the church would be and went directly to their prayer meeting. He knocked on the door, and a servant girl named Rhoda answered. She recognized Peter immediately and rushed to tell the church, leaving Peter outside. The church praying for Peter's release assumed the young servant girl was mistaken. Peter knocked again. Rhoda answered, and the same thing happened again! She was told that she had seen a ghost. It was easier for the church to believe in ghosts than that God had answered their prayers! The third time Peter knocked, he pushed his way in, and presented himself free to a shocked, praying church.

We pray in the church for people to be healed, and when it occasionally happens, we cannot believe it. We seldom pray specifically for the lost in our city, and then wonder why no lost show up at our revivals. God will not answer unprayed prayers. He does not empower faithless words. Real prayers produce extraordinary results, but ordinary prayer produces little power.

Jesus said in John 14, "Ask the Father what you will in my name and you will receive it." "In my name" is the key to powerful prayers.

Most of our prayers are simply a laundry list of what we think we need mixed with a whole lot of what we want. The good news is that God wants us to pray for our needs, but that should not be the entirety of our prayer life. We pull God off the prayer shelf when we need him or want something. When our children are sick, we plead with God for healing. When He answers, we forget all our promises. We promise more and more and then retract our promises when we get what we want. In fact, many go so far as to say that unless God gives us what we want, He is not answering our prayers.

Once, on an airplane radio station, I heard a famous atheist comedian's routine about prayer. He said, "I do not believe in God anymore because God does not answer my prayer. I decided to have a test. Each day for a month I asked God to give me a specific thing. I received the things I asked for about 15% of the time. For the next month, I prayed to a dead friend of mine. I received what I asked for about 25% of the time. Who needs God? I just pray to my friend Joe and get what I want with no strings attached."

That is a sad look at how most people view prayer. We pray for what we want, and if we do not get it, we accuse God of not really caring. We can ask God for anything. He is a loving Heavenly Father who loves to bestow good gifts. That should be a small portion of our prayer life, used only when we really need help. Our prayer should be, first and foremost, seeking to have a relationship with God.

Immanuel Scott, the great black preacher, told a story that drives this point home. Immanuel said, "My daughter returned home to live with us again and brought her three-year-old son with her. That grandson loved me and I loved him. Each morning I would arise early and go to the kitchen table to drink my coffee and read my paper. My grandson would join me soon, just to sit on my lap and lay his head on my shoulder. He just wanted to be with Grandpa. After I read my paper, I would eat breakfast, and my grandson joined me. He ate the same cereal the same way Grandpa did. After breakfast, I took a walk and he went with me just to be with Grandpa. Later I went to the mall with my wife, daughter, and grandson. My grandson found a pair of sneakers he wanted for $100. My wife said, 'Don't you spend no $100 on him.' My daughter said, 'Don't pay $100 for sneakers for this boy. We'll get some cheaper elsewhere.' I bought the sneakers. You see, most of the time my grandson didn't want nothing but to be with his Grandpa. So when he does ask me for something, I get it for him because he loves me."

When all our time with God is just selfish and not relational, we miss the point. Prayer is for building a relationship with the Father. When we have that kind of relationship and need a little power, He is right there for us.

Prayer is to seek His direction. Jesus prayed in Gethsemane, "Not my will but Thine be done." We spend way too much prayer time telling God what He needs to do, and how He needs to do it, rather than seeking what He has for us today. I believe God has a lot of good things to tell us about what He is up to and how to find the right direction, but we either don't tune in, or will not shut up long enough to hear the instructions (Jeremiah 33:3).

We must learn to listen to God in prayer. A wise man once said, "God gave us two eyes, two ears, two hands, two feet, and one tongue. Does that tell you something?" I think it does. It tells me I need to spend twice as much time listening to God than talking to God. "Well," you say, "God never talks to me!" Have you listened? The Father speaks to me all the time, not audibly, but rather in ways louder than that! The Father, through the Holy Spirit, speaks so loud, it is deafening within my spirit.

Prayer is power. The Holy Spirit will fill you with the power you need when you build your relationship with God in prayer.

Lastly, do what He says. Jesus prayed, "Not my will but yours be done" and then got up and went to the cross with all the power He needed to lay down His life.

Pray for direction and power and then get up and do it. Work the plan, get On Mission in Jerusalem and to the uttermost parts of the world. God has empowered you to get it done.

CHAPTER 5

STRATEGY FOR REACHING YOUR JERUSALEM

Reaching your Jerusalem begins when you catch God's vision for where you are. It includes recognizing that God wants and expects you to reach your Jerusalem and submitting to God's will. Second, it is the desire placed upon your heart for your Jerusalem. It is a fact that there are unbelievers in your Jerusalem, and it is a fact that God wants you to reach them! But have you caught the desire of God for your Jerusalem?

That desire must be kindled in you by the Holy Spirit of God. "You will receive power when the Holy Spirit has come upon you." The Holy Spirit will burn into your heart the desire to reach the unreachable in your Jerusalem. The Holy Spirit does this work differently in each person.

To some, He simply implants the truth of God's love for all people. That simple truth burns deep into some hearts to the extent that they can do nothing less than to reach out to their neighbors. To some, He implants the understanding of the reality of hell–that there are people in our Jerusalem who will spend eternity in hell unless we actively and consistently share the Gospel message with them. To others He shares the depth of God's love for all people. Some see the cross as a motivation that drives them to prolific spontaneous witnessing.

While a student at Southwestern Baptist Theological Seminary, I had the privilege of sitting in several classes taught by Dr. Roy Fish, Professor of Evangelism. He was not just a professor but also an evangelist. He walked his talk daily. I remember a story he told in class one day about the death of his prematurely born baby son. It was evident to the medical staff that this baby would not live long, so they encouraged Dr. Fish and his wife to hold the tiny infant as often as they could. Dr. Fish spoke of the emotion that filled him as he rocked that tiny infant for hours, weeping as he rocked. He questioned the strong emotions he was feeling for the child, because he had not known the infant long at all. He wept bitterly over the imminent death of this small stranger. Why such strong emotions over this tiny one? After hours of rocking and praying, he concluded that the most tragic part of it all was having so much love to give this little one that he would never know about. He would die before he would understand or experience the love of his father and family. Dr. Fish's heart was broken over this issue of unfulfilled love.

Likewise, God weeps bitter tears over the unfulfilled love He has for the lost in our Jerusalem. When the Spirit burns that into the hearts of people, they cannot help but witness to the lost of Jerusalem.

To others witnessing is an act of obedience. God commands it, so we must obey. There is no choice for the soldiers of the Lord's army. The commander speaks the order, and the soldiers follow the command. There is no further need of explanation, for duty demands it.

Yet others need more intense prodding. To these, the Holy Spirit brings conviction of failure. The guilt of disobedience or an uncaring spirit brings the reluctant disciple to roll call for duty. It is, indeed, sad to say that guilt alone drives many of God's chosen to bear reluctant witness to the lost in Jerusalem. Yet the Holy Spirit brings that conviction regularly because the task is too important to let it lay unfulfilled.

For far too many, however, none of these promptings of the Holy Spirit move us to faithful witnessing to our Jerusalem. Polls have repeatedly shown that generally less than 10% of Christians ever share their faith with another person. The desire or the will is simply absent or repressed in their lives. Their fear overcomes their faith to such an extent that they remain on the sidelines as the multitudes of their Jerusalem walk off into eternity lost. Indifference so dominates their lives that they will not be aroused by heaven's call; or worse, many who claim the name of Jesus have not truly been born again. Jesus said that after that the Holy Spirit comes you "will be my witnesses." The indwelling Holy Spirit gives us no choice, makes no exceptions. We witness because the Holy Spirit compels us to do so!

I gladly received Jesus Christ into my life as my personal Lord and Savior on November 11, 1958, at Chalkville Baptist Church, Chalkville, Alabama. I had always believed in Jesus, but that Sunday morning I truly understood that I had to receive Him personally. I ran down the aisle to take my pastor's hand with tears filling my eyes. At 11 years of age, I was wonderously saved. I told everyone at home and then called my grandparents and cousins. I wanted everybody to know Jesus was my Savior. The next day I told my teacher and at recess I took Nelson Bius under the hedges in our "fort" and told him about my experience. I explained what I had done and that he could do it too, so under the hedges I led Nelson in the sinner's prayer. I do not know if I said all those things correctly, but I knew I had to share with everyone I knew what had happened to me. It took me several months of watching other Christians to get "normal" and stop sharing! Yes, the normal thing is to sit there and do nothing. I began to notice that when the invitation was given some people even got up early to leave the service. It seems that a lot of Christians do not really get excited to see other people saved. However, the Bible says all of heaven rejoices whenever one lost person comes to Jesus (Luke 15:7). When we surrender ourselves to the Holy Spirit, He will move us to be a faithful witness for Him in our Jerusalem. When we catch the heart of God we cannot rest until we reach our Jerusalem for Christ. God has put each one of us in our Jerusalem to witness and win others to their heavenly Father, who loves each person.

I suggest that we covenant with God to win our Jerusalem to Him. A covenant is a binding legal and/or ethical agreement between two or more parties. For us it will become a binding promise that we openly and publically make to God to reach our Jerusalem for Him.

A covenant like this should have two functional levels. First, it is an intentional act of our will to promise God that we will take seriously His desire to reach our Jerusalem. I believe that to really develop an Acts 1:8 strategy we must do more than just agree in principle with the concept. To agree on principle says we know what God says; but that alone does not necessarily mean that it will move us to action. Again, I think that if we survey Christian people, they will agree that God wants to save the world; however that does not seem to motivate them to be a part of the process. Agreement is good, but agreement alone will not change a life. A covenant is when we intentionally decide to move on our agreement with God.

Through the years I have seen thousands of Christians trained in various methods of evangelism. They will come by the dozens to be trained, but on the day they are to go out and do the evangelism, most do not show up. The fact they came to be trained shows that they know what God expects, but the fact that they do not put it into practice shows that they have not been moved to action.

I want to encourage each of you, my readers, to make a covenant with God right now that not only will you agree with His view but that you will personally act upon your agreement. I suggest you write this covenant out, sign it, have it witnessed by two other individuals, and place it in a visible location as a reminder of your sacred covenant with God. Feel free to use this format as your covenant with God:

I _____your name_____ recognize that God's will is for everyone in _____your city_____ to come to faith in Jesus Christ as Lord and Savior.

I give my sacred promise to God that I will actively and continually witness in my city of my faith and salvation in Jesus Christ, with a view to win my city to Jesus.

Signed _____
Witness _____
Witness _____
Date _____

A sacred promise or covenant is very serious business and must not be taken lightly. Do not make this promise unless you are serious about your covenant (Ecc. 5:1-7). Why should you do the public covenant? Everyone God calls, He calls publicly and requires public follow-ship. Jesus called his disciples publicly, and He required them to follow Him publicly by leaving their jobs and houses to walk with Him.

Public commitment gives us needed accountability. Programs like Alcoholics Anonymous and Weight Watchers are often successful because they understand the effectiveness and power of personal accountability. We Christians must make ourselves accountable to other Christians in order to be more effective and consistent in our effort to reach our Jerusalem.

This first intentional step is an absolute must if you expect to really reach the Jerusalem where God has you planted. The second step is to lead your church to the same level of commitment.

The church will agree overwhelmingly with the concept of Acts 1:8, "reaching your Jerusalem," but they must be led to put that agreement into practice. Will everyone get on board with you in the covenant? Obviously not, but they must be led to public accountability by some method.

In every movie I have ever seen about the Alamo, there has been a scene when the commander drew a line on the ground with his sword and asked for a public commitment to stay and fight. Every man there understood that such a commitment would mean his probable death because the enemy overwhelmingly out-numbered them; yet almost every man stepped across that line to commit his life to the cause.

Why was this done publicly? Simply put, it made each man accountable for his decision. This accountability gave even the most faint-hearted the strength to carry on.

All of us need accountability in our lives. It is part of God's plan for our lives, and it is necessary to keep most of us going. Even the strongest of us grow weak from time to time. I remember a cartoon from years ago that really speaks to this need for accountability.

A woman is standing at the door of the bedroom speaking to her husband who is still lying in bed.

"It is time to get up and go to church," said she.

"I'm not going to church today," said the husband as he pulled the covers defiantly over his head.

"Oh, yes you are!" demanded the wife. "Why don't you want to go?"

"I'm too tired, and besides, no one likes me down there at that church. Tell me one good reason I should go," he responded.

"Because you are the pastor!" came the terse reply.

What would we do without the accountability of our spouses? All of us need to stay accountable in every area of our lives, especially in the area of personal evangelism/witnessing. Our churches need a public accountability of their intent to reach their Jerusalem and an ongoing accountability to get it done.

Plan a worship service that will conclude with an opportunity for the congregation to make a public commitment to reach their Jerusalem. This commitment service could include signing a covenant similar to the one we shared before, and then bringing those covenants forward to lay on the altar. The service should emphasize a covenant commitment as a sacred promise to God that must not be taken lightly.

This service could be followed up by an official vote of the church to accept the covenant with God, stating the commitment to the Acts 1:8 strategy. This official covenant should be publically displayed and published in all church publications.

Several years ago, I led my church to adopt a new vision statement that was similar to these Acts 1:8 covenants. This statement was adopted by the whole church: "We covenant with God to aggressively become a model great commission church." We published this vision in all our publications and began each worship service by repeating the statement. We continually emphasized that this was a sacred promise we had made with God. Keeping these commitments before the congregation enables the church to prioritize missions in church life.

To reach your Jerusalem, mission involvement must be the priority in the church psyche and programs.

Prioritize missions in the church budget. Someone once pointed out that you can tell where a man's heart is by looking at his checkbook. Likewise, you can tell where the heart of a church is by looking at its budget. The vast majority of church budgets will reflect a greater concern about operations and programs than about reaching our Jerusalem and beyond.

Add together all the money budgeted for Cooperative Program, associational missions, and other mission evangelism activities, and figure the percentage of the total church budget used for those purposes. In many churches the percentage will be less than 10% to mission evangelism commitment.

In order to make missions a true priority this percentage will need to be between 25% and 40%. If we are going to take seriously our commitment covenant with God, we are going to have to put our money where our mouth is. The rule is quite simple: if a church does not finance missions, then missions will not happen to the degree necessary to win your Jerusalem to Jesus. Prioritize your church budget to emphasize missions.

Prioritize your church program to make it a real Acts 1:8 church. What does your church program reflect as the priority of your church? Take some time to carefully review the programs your church consistently emphasizes. Is missions a consistent part of your Sunday School program and worship services? These two programs draw the largest attendance in your church. Are these programs fully and consistently a place where missions are highlighted and emphasized? To really prioritize the Acts 1:8 strategy, a consistent part of these programs must be dedicated to innovative missions emphasis. As you look at your weekday programs, is there a consistent mission emphasis by providing varied mission action opportunities, challenging your people to serve in your Jerusalem, or does most of your weekday preparation simply pull people back to the church and away from their Jerusalem? Is there a real effort to open your church regularly to your Jerusalem? To what extent does the church have its

Jerusalem coming to it, and the church serving in its Jerusalem? Again, most often our programs simply show the church serving and going back to the church!

We cannot reach our Jerusalem from behind church walls. Either Jerusalem must come inside the church or the church must be found consistently in Jerusalem–preferably both. How does your church intentionally find itself in your Jerusalem, and how effective are the programs that you do in your Jerusalem?

Prioritize mission education for all age levels in your church. How will God's people know God's heart about missions if they are not trained?

As Jesus trained His disciples He taught them daily about missions as He led them daily in Jerusalem. Everywhere Jesus went, He took His disciples with Him so that they could see first-hand how He loved Jerusalem and needed to reach it. Jesus literally lived in His Jerusalem as He touched people's lives all day every day, educating His disciples to be prepared when they received the Acts 1:8 command. The disciples knew exactly what to do and how to do it when the Spirit came upon them. They simply mimicked what Jesus did.

They preached, healed, taught, and touched people because that is how Jesus had trained them. In like manner, churches must train their people to do missions as Jesus did missions. Mission education is a vital link in mobilizing our people to be Acts 1:8 Christians. My heart for missions began early in my life. My mother consistently taught me and showed me a mission heart. I grew up in a church that emphasized missions through programs like Sunbeams, Royal Ambassadors, Girls in Action, Women's Missionary Union, and Brotherhood. These programs trained me from my earliest memory as to how important missions really are to God and to the church.

When I became a pastor, I had already been well trained, so I just revisited what I had lived out in my home church. Had I not been educated so well in my childhood, pastoring with an Acts 1:8 mentality would have been much more difficult. The church today must educate all our people concerning missions. We cannot expect Christians to learn missions by osmosis; education must be intentional and effective.

The best mission education will always be involvement in missions, or on-the-job training. Children can do missions, and they will enjoy doing mission projects. My children have been involved in missions all their lives. They went with me locally and globally, and participated with great enthusiasm in all aspects of missions. They helped "teach" in Backyard Bible Clubs, they handed out Scripture and tracts, and they visited nursing homes and shut-ins. These were not chores, but times of great enjoyment. Rather than eliminating mission action among your children's programs, escalate them!

Churches should have a constant flow of missionaries visiting the church. This contact with all types of missionaries will educate the congregation and help produce a missions heart. This mission heart is necessary to reach the Jerusalem they live in, so prioritize mission education in your church.

Prioritize missions in your church by praying consistently over your Jerusalem. Prayer, of course, is the heart of mission involvement. We will become concerned over what we pray for, and we pray for what concerns us most. Allow me to suggest some ways to pray effectively over your Jerusalem:

1. Pray over every name in your telephone directory. Now, if you live in Atlanta, Georgia, or Dallas, Texas, and have only a couple of hundred people in your church, this will be a monumental task; however, if you live in Dothan, Alabama, or Martin, Tennessee, and have a thousand members, it will be a simple process. Collect several telephone books and tear the pages out. Give each member a page, and ask them to pray over each name individually. This process may take several weeks or months, but ask the congregation to faithfully pray for some of the people each day until all are thoroughly covered in prayer. Then ask them to mail a prayer card to each person on their page. The prayer card should say, "I have been praying for you and your family," and signed by the person with the church name included. This process, again, might require several weeks or months, but

the process can continue until all the names in the directory have been prayed over. Then repeat the process to keep prayer for your Jerusalem a priority.

2. Do prayer walking around your city or specific areas of your city. Again, if you live in Los Angeles, this will be a greater task than if you live in Fitzgerald, Georgia, but both can be profitable. Break down your city into blocks, or streets, and assign the small pieces to individual families to prayer walk. It might be good to assign each block or street to two families, so that some accountability can be assured. Prayer walking teams should be trained in the "how to" of successful prayer walking. Each team should stop in front of every house and pray for each inhabitant of that house. Pray specifically for the salvation and openness to a Gospel presentation. If residents are in the yard, or visible, tell them that you are praying for every house on their street and ask for any special needs they may have so they can be included in the prayer time. If the prayer team knows the people in the house, then visit with them to seek special prayer requests.

3. You might also consider prayer walking specific public areas like schools, malls, and government buildings. These prayer walking experiences can be a bonding activity for members as well as families. The prayer walking should be an organized effort where you train the teams to be very specific and very intentional in their prayer efforts.

4. Your prayer walking strategy needs to be a continual program, not just a one-time event. The prayer walking should be unashamedly evangelistic in its nature. Prayer walkers must pray for the salvation of the Jerusalem in general, and specifically for the area where they are assigned to prayer walk. It might be necessary to rotate the areas that teams prayer walk to make sure that all your city is covered by prayer.

The next step in reaching your Jerusalem should be to canvas your city to find out its real makeup and to determine how best to reach it.

In almost all cities there will be ethnic pockets of people, economic differences, and cultural preferences. These need to be identified in order to be more effective in our efforts to win Jerusalem.

Canvassing your city might take several different directions, or a combination of several methods.

1. The traditional method is door-to-door teams who personally question residents as to their spiritual situation. This is a very effective canvassing method, but it might be too large a task, depending on the size of your city and/or the size of your church.

2. Door-to-door canvassing can be supplemented by telephone canvassing. Senior Adults especially are able and willing to help out in telephone canvassing. This allows information to be gathered more conveniently.

3. State Conventions can provide LASERS (1), PROBE (2), and demographics (3) to help your church get a better understanding of your Jerusalem.

A LAZER (1) is a hands-on approach to identify embedded language people groups in a certain area for the purpose of starting an ethnic church.

A PROBE (2) is a hands-on approach to identify Anglo populations in need of a new work.

Demographics (3) is composed of statistical material about your local area, including population make-up and characteristics.

The information gleaned from these canvassing efforts should be used to develop an intentional plan to locate and reach the lost of your Jerusalem. Plans should be developed as an overall strategy to target specific areas with specific events and/or methods designed specifically for each people or culture group discovered. While it is true that one method of evangelism will not fit every situation, general evangelistic principles do apply to every people group or culture group. The information you receive from your canvassing is very important, but it is only as good as your use of the information to reach people with the Gospel.

We will share the Gospel with our Jerusalem house to house, person to person (Acts 20:20). This must be the absolute commitment of every Acts 1:8 Christian and church. Therefore, there must be a definite strategy to:

1. Reach the lost of our Jerusalem. Lostness is not acceptable to an Acts 1:8 Christian or church. It is God's will for all to be saved. We may not see everyone in our Jerusalem saved, but we must present to everyone the personal opportunity to be saved. It is not enough to have an open door policy at your church. It will only be enough when Acts 1:8 Christians go through those doors to intentionally confront our Jerusalem with the message of salvation in Jesus Christ. This will not happen accidentally, but it can happen as we set our intentional strategy to evangelize our Jerusalem. Preaching, teaching, door-to-door witnessing, Scripture distribution, evangelistic events, and direct involvement in Jerusalem must be continuously applied to identify and reach people for Jesus.

2. Invite the unchurched to be actively involved in your church. All unchurched people need to churched. The church is the Bride of Christ, founded by Christ as a place of worship, service, growth, and discipleship. The church was not an afterthought of Jesus, but a central requirement needed by every saved person. Acts 1:8 churches must be so compelling by their love (John 13:35) that the unchurched will be drawn to church as a moth is drawn to a light. Acts 1:8 churches must be compelling.

A compelling church reflects the love of Christ, not the strife of the world. I am afraid that many, if not most, of our churches are not compelling. I visit many churches in my ministry, and I must admit that most are not compelling, but rather provoke the response, "Why in the world would I want to go there?" If our churches are not compelling to believers, how could they be compelling to the unchurched?

How does an Acts 1:8 church become a church that will compel the unchurched to come? It will not be by becoming like the world, nor competing with the world. The church is not to become an entertainment center, talent show, a theater of fine arts, or a recreation facility. The church is compelling when it is the church where there is a distinct recognizable difference from the world. Jesus said to be "salt and light" (Matthew 5:13-16). Salt is a preservative and antiseptic to raw skin. Light is bright and exposes everything. Both salt and light can be unpleasant to some, but it is their saltiness and brightness that allows them to be most effective. The Acts 1:8 church must not surrender its saltiness and its brightness, lest it surrender its main reason for existence. When worship becomes mere entertainment it ceases to be Biblical worship. When a church becomes so self-centered that it never dirties itself in its Jerusalem, it fails the test of Biblical authority. When a church becomes so like the world that members bear no marks of discipleship, it ceases to be compelling. In 2004, for the first time in church history there were more divorces in the church than in the world. The church, indeed, will be compelling only when it becomes like the New Testament church.

3. Discover the needs in our Jerusalem. As we aggressively share the Gospel in our Jerusalem with the lost and unchurched, we will discover many needs. These needs will require active ministry from your church. It is obvious that there are many hurting people in our Jerusalem. People are suffering not only spiritually, but emotionally and physically as well. Jesus often dealt with these needs as He moved in ministry among the people. He was moved to compassion time and time again as he ministered to the crowds. Jesus often performed physical miracles to transform the lives of the people around Him, but He also touched them where they hurt emotionally and mentally. Jesus demonstrated a unique kind of gentle love as He touched people. This love was offered to everyone with whom He made contact. Jesus modeled this love in His ministry, and it is the ministering love that the church must share if we will reach our Jerusalem. Jesus commanded us to feed the hungry, clothe the naked, and visit the lonely and disenfranchised just as He did. If we are to truly reach our Jerusalem it will be when we learn to lovingly and consistently minister to our community.

At our church in Albany we made a day care program available to our entire Jerusalem. We often had as many as 200 little ones on our campus each weekday. I would often go to the rooms and talk with the children, especially the three-year-olds.

I would sit on the floor and just listen to them "talk" to me. Always one or two would come and sit in my lap without being invited. They would chatter away, seeking my attention as they shared their precious lives with me. Soon more would come and get as close as they could to me, vying for the attention they wanted so badly. Invariably there would be one or two shy ones who would just stand to the side and look at my interaction with their playmates. Sometimes I would wave them over to sit next to me and give them special attention. Some would hug me and get as close to me as possible. I always felt so sad that some of these precious little ones might not have a male role model in their lives. For a few fleeting moments I was the Daddy they needed so much.

There are so many people who need to be able to receive a hug from Daddy. The good news is that our Heavenly Father has hugs for all who need it, but He often allows us the privilege of being the "hugger" for Him.

One might rightfully ask, "How could I hug my community?" As you go door to door and telephone to telephone, or person to person, and a need becomes evident, then mobilize your church to meet that need.

When people are hungry, feed them.

When people are in need of clothes, provide clothing.

When people need advice, counsel them.

When people have special needs, provide support groups for the widowed, divorced, abused, pregnant, new moms, and diseased, and have people who are lonely to visit them.

At my last pastorate our staff had a daily hospital visitation schedule. We often would have people who were not members of our church put our church down on their hospital registration as their church, because they knew they would get a visit each day. Lonely people are everywhere. Reach out and touch them with compassion.

When people are newcomers to your city, provide them with information about community services such as doctors, schools, and cultural opportunities.

Another great way to reach your Jerusalem is through specific, timely Scripture distribution. For example, on Easter, Christmas, Memorial Day, Valentine's Day, and other holidays, give out Scripture portions door to door, or person to person, highlighting that particular holiday or emphasis. People are much more likely to read a Scripture portion that they see as relevant for the occasion. Scripture is the power of God, and it will speak to people's hearts long after the visit or contact is over. Our job is to just get the Word into their hands and allow the Holy Spirit to do His work.

A wonderful way to make personal contact, especially in a larger Jerusalem, is to set up telephone committees to call the community. These could be as simple as "May I pray for you today?" or a survey. The telephone is still a great tool to let people know who you are, and that you really do care.

The Bible requires that we not only reach the reachable, but that we hunt down the difficult. Jesus put it like this in Luke 14:23: "And the master said to the slave, 'Go out into the highways and along the hedges, and compel them to come in, so that my house may be filled.'"

The highways and hedges were the places where people went who did not especially want to be found. Oh, yes, God wants us to locate the "unreachable" because even they can be reached by the power of God.

An elderly man in my church lost his wife of 55 years. He would often come to visit me in my office to remember the times they had together. He would always end his visit by reminding me that although he had many widows offering to fulfill his life, he just was not interested in another woman. This continued for well over a year. One day he visited me to ask me if I would officiate at his wedding. I met his "intended" and told her his story. Her response was simple, "He had not met me yet!"

Many of the unreached have not met Jesus yet, but when they meet Him face to face, they will not be so unreachable after all!

Consider the unreachableness of the Apostle Paul, Eldridge Cleaver, C. S. Lewis, and others. God still changed their lives. The question then arises, "How can we reach them?"

I believe that the FAITH training program is not only an excellent tool to train our people in evangelism, but a great way to put them in their Jerusalem with the good news of Christ. It is a Sunday School based church outreach program, and is available through your State Baptist Convention, or Lifeway. The FAITH survey is an excellent tool and very simple to use. We have put teams in malls and on streets with just five simple questions that enable you to quickly move to a FAITH presentation.

Event evangelism is yet another opportunity to reach your Jerusalem. Event evangelism is an event designed especially to reach and impact the community. These events can be held at the church, or in a community house. Circuses, game day, mission fairs, movie theaters, Easter egg hunts, and famous speakers or singers can be used to draw the community into hearing our message about Jesus.

Revivals can still be used to reach the community, but not just revival as usual. These meetings must be carefully and intensely focused on the unbelieving community. There is no substitute for members bringing their lost friends, but members often do not have lost friends or are not motivated to bring them to church. Revivals that reach the lost must use some means that will interest the community to make an effort to come and inspire the membership to invite the lost to the services. Often you can encourage the community by recognizing the service people of the community. (For example, one night to recognize and honor the police; another to target firefighters and EMTs (Emergency Medical Technicians); another night, health care workers.) These services must be sincere and honest efforts to reward and encourage service personnel. Special presentations and awards should be offered. It is important to realize that just inviting these people will not guarantee their attendance. You must build a rapport with them and work hard to get them to the service. Teachers in public schools, public work officials and food service personnel are also great target groups to invite for special love and fellowship seminars.

Many churches are also successful in reaching people by having a magician evangelist, weightlifting exhibitions, or professional athletes as a draw to the community. These activities must target the lost community, but the lost will be won by your care, love, and attention when they visit and you follow-up.

Good old-fashioned visitation works especially in the "hedges". To reach our unreached people we must go where we might not ordinarily visit. Mobile home parks, apartments, and public housing areas are full of people who need to meet the Father and to see His love in us. You might start house Bible studies in their areas in order to reach the people where they are. To truly reach our Jerusalem there must not be any place where our church will not go to touch people with the Gospel. The down-and-outs and the up-and-comers all need the love of Jesus, and the church must follow up on their decisions.

Every plan and every activity in our Jerusalem must develop a follow-up strategy. It is not good enough to touch and run, or win them and drop them. To reach our Jerusalem we must develop disciples of all those we touch and reach. This is probably the biggest area of failure in our churches. We plan events and programs well, but we often drop the ball in follow-up. This is similar to rejoicing over the birth of a baby, and then walking away to let him raise himself. The end result of this strategy is death. Evangelism without follow-up is irresponsibility. Plan strategically for follow-up.

Disciple the saved. Encourage, motivate, and nurture those new births in Christ. Do not give up or give in. Keep after them, regardless of the cost or time involved. The keys are love and consistency. If they will not come to the church to be discipled, then go to their house. Be innovative with interesting presentations, not boring and predictable! A daily walk with Jesus is an exciting growth experience. Teach them to pray. Teach them the thrill of personal Bible study. Show them the joy of Christian fellowship. Plug them in to radiant Christians who will patiently love them all the way to maturity.

Develop a backup plan for your follow-up. This will mean walking the second and third mile. You might have to shift personnel to find someone who "clicks" with them, or someone more their age, or with similar interests. You might have to take them out to lunch, or to a ball game, or watch their child in a school play before they will give you the privilege of discipling them.

There might be a need to refer a new believer or a prospect to a ministry team. As Jesus taught us, it is hard to understand the Bread of Heaven when you need a loaf of bread to satisfy your physical hunger. Sometimes we reach people by kind, loving acts of Christian ministry. As we minister to their physical need or emotional need, we gain the right to minister to them spiritually. Follow-up is essential to an Acts 1:8 church. After Acts 1:8 came Pentecost, and after Pentecost came follow-up: "They were continually devoting themselves to the apostles' teaching and to fellowship, to the breaking of bread, and to prayer" (Acts 2:42).

CHAPTER 6

STRATEGY FOR REACHING YOUR JUDEA

Our Acts 1:8 equivalent for Judea is the state where your church is located. As Acts 1:8 people and churches, we must be very concerned with the spiritual condition of our state. The state of Georgia where I reside is in the well-known Bible Belt, but it is still 70% unchurched and unsaved. The reasons for such a staggering figure are varied.

One, although Georgia Christians are evangelizing their state regularly, they are not keeping up with the population growth. Two, the world is moving to Georgia. Ethnic, non-Christian populations are skyrocketing in Georgia. Three, churches are not aggressively finding ways to reach people in Georgia, and finally, Christians are indifferent to the lostness of our state. What are we to do? Acts 1:8 commands that we must reach our Judea for Jesus, so Acts 1:8 people must make a renewed commitment to reach our Judea.

We commit to partner within our state to reach a group of people in a location for Jesus Christ. We know we cannot reach all the people of our state but we commit to partner with others to do a more effective job of reaching our state for Christ.

First, we need a partnership strategy to make sure all of our state is effectively saturated with the Gospel. A strategic plan is a plan that we can participate in that allows the most effective use of our time, talent and resources.

Your state convention might already have a strategic plan in place, so start by contacting your State Convention Volunteer office.

Second, decide how your talents and the talents of your church can best be used in reaching the state for Jesus.

1. Perhaps there are some large cities in your state where you can become involved for evangelistic endeavors. You can work through your state convention or the association office where that large city is located to see what is presently being done.

2. Perhaps you can partner with a church in that large city to help them in special projects or evangelistic activities in the city.

3. Your talent might be better used in a rural type setting. Again, a good place to start is with your state convention or the association in the area where you feel led to serve.

4. In every state there will be recreational areas where you can go to do evangelistic type ministry. These might include providing Vacation Bible School teams, or Bible Studies in local homes, or showing religious films in resort locations.

It is important to have an idea of the kind of work that you are led of God to follow. After the initial decision, then make a vision trip by yourself, or with your key leadership, to see firsthand what can be done, and what the most pressing needs are. At this time you can discover camps, colleges, or motels that can be used by your team, as well as other logistics, such as transportation and food availability. You can also coordinate with local associations and churches to make a joint plan.

Many of the same activities you use in your Jerusalem will be just as effective in your Judea, but sometimes you will have to be innovative and flexible.

After you make the vision trip, then get ready to recruit your team, or teams.

Cast the vision before the potential team member. Casting the vision is a very important part of your strategy and should be prayerfully delivered. Start with the vision for an Acts 1:8 strategy. We are responsible for our Judea. Jesus commanded us to go to our Jerusalem and do our best to saturate Judea with the Gospel. People are moved by need, so the needs you have discovered must be the center of the vision.

People are lost, unchurched, and have little hope without the Acts 1:8 person, church, or association of churches. Tell the potential team how they can meet that specific need as they go.

Explain how the team will make an impact on the area and the people to be saved.

Next, explain the event or missions in detail. How long it will last, how much it will cost, and how the goal will be accomplished.

Explain how the team will incorporate evangelism into this event. The heart and soul of each mission opportunity should be evangelism. However, evangelism can be done in numerous ways.

Also explain what will be expected from each team member. Will they share their testimony, hand out tracts, counsel people who have made decisions, or share from a marked New Testament? Each member needs to feel confident in the methodology chosen, but everyone will be expected to use the opportunity to do evangelism.

Next, talk about the absolute importance of discipleship and follow-up. Follow-up must be implanted in the team members' minds before they ever commit to be on mission in Judea. If follow-up is to be done by a local church, the plan must be fully in place before the trip begins.

Again, talk about a specific plan, not "We will leave the follow-up to the local people." Be specific. For example: "The local church will have a six week Bible course for every person who has made a decision for Christ, or the church will use the *Survival Kit for New Christians*, and do personal instruction in the homes for each individual."

It is important to get a financial deposit from each person who wants to go to Judea. Many people will be moved by the vision but fail to follow through with the commitment.

At the same time of the financial commitment, get a commitment for training. Unless members are willing to be trained, they cannot go with the team. Depending on the ability of the team the training could take one to three sessions, but set your goal to have your Judean team to be well informed and well trained.

Now, you are ready to give special attention to your event. It has been correctly stated, "To fail to plan is to plan to fail." Your plan should be thorough, yet simple. A good plan begins with the purpose of the event. What do you really desire to see accomplished on this event?

*Example: We will partner with First Baptist Church Crossroads to have six simultaneous Backyard Bible clubs in the area of Jones Road to share the Gospel with 100 children by lovingly demonstrated Biblical principles, and stories as each team member models his or her faith to the children. Each child will receive a **Survival Kit** and personal follow-up in their home by the First Baptist Church Crossroads team.*

Next, decide the best methods you can use to be successful in accomplishing the project.

1. We will have six trained teams made up of four of our members and three members from First Baptist Church Crossroads.

2. Our team will do the Bible stories, music, and puppets, and First Baptist Church Crossroads will lead the crafts and provide the refreshments.

3. Each team member will use this year's standard Vacation Bible School material and cover two lessons each day for five days. Materials for all teams will be provided by us.

4. The team will gather for prayer at 8:00 AM, and the Vacation Bible School will last from 8:30 AM until 11:30 AM.

Then you must determine what materials will be used for the project. Again, it is important to take more than enough materials with you. It is always better to have too much than too few. There needs to be enough tracts, Scriptures, and other material to last the entire project time. If you are doing Vacation Bible School or Backyard Bible Clubs, crafts are especially important. You do not want to have your team out looking for materials after you arrive.

It is important to know the possibilities at the site in order to prepare accurately.

It is also important to try to have a good balance on your team. If there are youth involved, it is very important to have adequate adult supervision. Youth make excellent mission trip participants, but they need mature adults to keep them focused on the task at hand. A mission experience is an excellent opportunity to blend a mixture of ages. As a rule, senior adults work extremely well with youth, and this enables the youth to get to know and respect the seniors. As Acts 1:8 leaders, you need to think about the composition of the team so that the experience will be of great benefit to each participant.

Again, plan your follow-up. Do not take follow-up for granted. It is not automatic. In fact, effective follow-up will make the experience worthwhile.

Follow-up can be immediate. You can take material with you to use as follow-up and actively enlist new believers in local New Testament churches. From day one begin following up on new believers. Start them in New Believer material, Bible study, and prayer. Enlist local churches in advance and set up a plan to incorporate the new believers in local fellowships.

Then get on with the actual event. The planning is all behind, you have done all the necessary work; now you can enjoy the experience itself. You have done all you can do to prepare to make this event worthwhile and Kingdom honoring. So, be flexible. This is the key word and attitude for all mission endeavors. It is not likely, but it is possible that everything might change when you arrive. Be flexible. It is highly likely that some things will most assuredly be different. Be flexible. You are going on this event to build the Kingdom, so Satan will oppose your efforts, or God might have a better idea. Be flexible. A flexible tree will survive any storm, but a rigid tree will fall. Be flexible. Train your team to be flexible. Prepare them from the beginning to expect the unexpected and be prepared to change a little, or all of their programs. Sometimes a greater victory comes when our plans fall by the wayside and God shows up in power.

Also do not let last-minute changes or cancellations prevent you from making the trip. If your desire is to serve God and build the Kingdom, then God will show up and lift you up.

We once sent a team to Idaho on a mission trip. All the plans were made, including reservation at the local motel. Upon arrival it was discovered that the motel had sold out and dropped our reservations. Quickly we met with the local pastor and arranged for housing with congregation members and friends. One friend

71

was an unsaved couple who were willing to help out with housing, having two empty bedrooms. After a week of housing these Acts 1:8 Christians the couple received Christ. This was an unexpected work of God which would not have happened had the team stayed in the motel.

Another time on a trip to Moldova our Christian van driver was unavailable to drive the team. A non-believer was substituted, even though he did not want to drive Christians. After four days he prayed to receive Christ and was a changed man. God can and does do wonderful things when it seems like things are collapsing. Be flexible, and watch what God can do.

DO THE FOLLOW-UP.

Use the last day of the trip, or immediately upon arrival home, to evaluate the trip. Have the leader debrief each of the team members and do a written follow-up.

Send the follow-up to your state convention, the partnering church and your leadership. This follow-up should report what went right and what went wrong. It should be as comprehensive as possible in order to aid the planning of the next event.

Your Judea is an important part of God's Kingdom strategy. It can very easily be overlooked or skipped, but a real Acts 1:8 person, church, or association will make sure that Judea is part of the Acts 1:8 strategy.

CHAPTER 7

STRATEGY FOR REACHING YOUR SAMARIA

The United States is our Samaria, and it is an awesome Samaria in many ways. The overwhelming size, scope, and diversity of the United States is both intimidating and exciting. The world has come to America, and the fields are ripe unto harvest. Representatives of almost every ethnic group around the world are now present in the United States, and they are usually more open to the Gospel here than they would be in their own countries. Our population centers range from some of the largest cities in the world to extremely rural areas. There are mountain people and beach people, and they all need the Gospel of Jesus. Acts 1:8 people will recognize this as one of God's great opportunities in the United States. Obviously one individual, one church, or one association cannot reach the vast country called the United States, but together, individuals can partner with others to cover our Samaria with the Gospel.

Partnering is the key: Acts 1:8 people joining together with one cause to win the United States to Jesus. Evangelization is the key: we must get the Gospel to every high-rise apartment and every crossroads in America. Each year Southern Baptists join together before our national convention for a "Crossover." Literally hundreds of Southern Baptists go early to the Convention site to join with local churches to cover that city with the message of Jesus. This kind of partnering always reaps great results. It is a micro-version of how effective partnering can be. One great strength of the church is our strength as we work together. It is called cooperation. When we cooperate financially and physically, there are literally no limits to our possibilities.

Step one, then, to reaching our Samaria is to join in partnership with other Acts 1:8 people. We acknowledge that we cannot do it all ourselves, but we understand that together in Acts 1:8 partnering, following God's leadership, we can make a significant difference.

Step two is to focus on one area. The key is focus. The needs are overwhelming everywhere. There is no state or city in the United States that does not need help. Rather than throwing up your hands in frustration, focus on one area or a few areas. Georgia Baptists are focused on New York, California, and Idaho-Utah. These are the areas we have chosen as our Samaria. It is not that we view them as more important or more needy than others, but that we have chosen these to focus on. We are calling out Acts 1:8 people to join in an effort to cover these states with the Good News. These states have vast opportunities with a ripe harvest field. For example, the fields in New York range from New York City's (more than) ten million people to small villages in western New York with only a few dozen people. God is ready to plug you in where your talent and materials can best be used. The key is focus.

Set a long-term goal to work with a specific area until that area is evangelized. For Los Angeles or San Diego or Salt Lake City, that could take years, but for Shasta and Elk City, that could be accomplished in a matter of months in an Acts 1:8 partnership.

Step three involves innovation. Train your teams to try new things. In some areas some evangelistic efforts will not be successful, but God will open a door to get the message out. Learning to think "out of the box" is an essential to effective partnering. Be willing to do whatever it takes for as long as it takes to reach Samaria.

Step four is to step out. Go, ready to demonstrate love to the people. They will be won to Christ, not by our talents or slick programs, but by our concern. That love might have to be proven by giving again and again. We might have to build relationships and prove our concern to earn the right to share. Most people will respond to honest, truthful, and loving efforts, but we must be willing to put in the time.

Where should you go in Samaria? This is often a difficult decision because there is so much need and opportunity. Who should you respond to? Again, I believe Acts 1:8 partnerships are the key.

We must join in as part of a plan and then work that plan. You can be effective going on your own, but you can be even more effective by being part of a group with a plan and a strategy. Like-minded people working together will make a tremendous impact on an area. Following up on that impact can leave an area capable of self-motivation and effectiveness.

Take a vision trip to a partnering area. See the needs and opportunities with your own eyes. Talk to workers in that area and hear their hearts. Pray for God to place you in your niche so you can be the most effective worker possible.

Then claim your vision. Make it personal and drive it hard and heart first. This is your Samaria, your niche that God has given you, and you will do all you can under God to be effective.

Count the costs. Are you willing to pay the price for the success God wants you to have? Success may not look as you thought. It might look like hundreds of people receiving Christ, or it might look like training local preachers and leaders to be more effective. It might look like a new church building, or a new coat of paint on a store-front church. It might look like a new church plant, or following up on discipling new believers. Success is measured by our willingness to go and be available to what God is doing.

Now that God has led you to your Samaria, let us look at the steps involved in getting there.

Make your contact with the people you will partner with. This might be your state office, who will put you in touch with a local pastor, church, or association.

Begin praying with your people and the people you will work with in Samaria. People matter. Let your state volunteer mission office meet with you both to set a strategy.

Train your team and ask the people on the other end to train their people to know how to work as partners. Partnership is the key. It must come equally from both directions. In fact, some of the greatest impacts made might just come from the relationship between team and host. This might set the table for real success to follow. All people workers need to be trained and refreshed on new areas.

Train your team to focus on Samaria. You are going there to help them do what God has planted them there to do. Mission team members make short-term trips to help enhance or enable the indigenous to do the work of the Lord.

It is very important that the mission team not take over from the locals, but help them in their task for the Lord.

It is always good to get prayer partners for the trip. Each individual team member and the locals should enlist as many prayer partners as they can enlist.

Next, make the trip with a joyful smile, a flexible attitude, and eyes open for every opportunity to share your faith in the Lord Jesus.

Do the event faithfully. Keep in mind that you are there to assist the locals and you are willing to do whatever they ask with joy. Again, do not just stick with the script, but look for everyday opportunities to share the joy of Christ at your hotel where you stay as well as at the event.

Reap the results. Take in every moment so that it will be with you all of your life. Create wonderful memories of your service to God. Carefully counsel with every person who shows any interest in a decision for Christ in any way.

Do as much follow-up as you can while you are there, and make arrangement with locals to do follow-up on every decision. Every decision is a person who God loves dearly. Then follow-up on the follow-up to make sure it is done.

When you get home, do a debriefing with the whole team to share experiences, and then make plans to share with the whole church and individual groups.

Then, start planning for your next trip, and start enlisting people to go with you. It is good to have those plans ready while enthusiasm is high. You might now begin to think about expanding your vision to include the "uttermost parts of the world."

CHAPTER 8

STRATEGY FOR REACHING THE UTTERMOST PARTS OF THE WORLD

"The uttermost parts of the world" is a phrase that excites hundreds of people, and brings chill bumps of fear to hundreds of others. To some, this idea of foreign missions is the only way to do missions, and to others it is a waste of time and energy that would be better used closer to home.

If one is to be an Acts 1:8 person, then foreign missions is a vital part of an overall Biblical worldview that cannot be overlooked. Acts 1:8 people, churches, and associations must have a Biblical worldview in order to be successful in setting up their mission plan.

The worldview of the Bible, and therefore of God, is laid out simply in John 3:16a, "For God so loved the world..." All the people of the world are loved by God who wants them all to be redeemed back to Himself. Nothing less than the church's 100% effort to reach the world for God through Jesus is acceptable to God.

There is not one person in this world that God does not desire to save. Not all people will be saved, but all people should have the opportunity to hear the Gospel and receive Jesus Christ as Lord. If this is not your worldview, then you need to adjust your view to God's view. Each one of us is held accountable to reach the world. It is not somebody else's job; it is ours.

Who are the people in the "uttermost parts of the world"? For our Acts 1:8 definition these are all the people outside the United States of America. That incorporates a large amount of people. Of course, we all know that is too many people for one person to reach for Jesus; however, we can, and must, partner with other Acts 1:8 people to be effective in getting the Gospel to them all. How?

1. We must pray for the salvation of the world.
2. We must pray for others to go.
3. We must encourage others to go.
4. We must enable others to go.
5. We must go ourselves
6. We must partner with others who are going.

Only when we do all these things are we truly Acts 1:8 people.

Why should we go? That is a good question worthy of a Biblical response.

1. God said so. Isaiah 45:22; Romans 14:11
2. Jesus said so. Acts 1:7-8
3. The Bible says so. Philippians 2:10-11
4. The disciples modeled it. Acts 13, 14; Acts 15:7; Acts 28:28

How shall we decide where to start our "uttermost" mission? Our decision must be:

1. Bathed in prayer.
2. Saturated in need.
3. Enhanced in partnership.

Please do not be a lone wolf, but be a part of our Acts 1:8 team. Again, by working cooperatively we can be so much more effective. The time is too short and this task is too large to do it our way by ourselves. The good that you do as an individual or church can be multiplied when you partner with other Acts 1:8 people.

As you set your prayer strategy, you will most likely be overwhelmed by the need "out there." There is so much to be done and such great need that there might be a tendency to back off and say "too much." Rather than react in fear or frustration, do a needs evaluation, letting the Holy Spirit tug at your heart.

Make contact with your state volunteer mission office and let them help you make your first contact with the area you have chosen. Or they may give you information about present needs in current partnerships. Think partnering for effectiveness.

Plan your strategy:

1. Where do we want to go?
2. Who do we want to reach?
3. How can we best reach these people with the assets (people, talent, time, money, and other help) we have?
4. How many people will be needed ?
5. How long will we need to be there?
6. How many trips will be needed?
7. How can we be most effective in follow-up?
8. How will this grow God's kingdom?
9. How much will it cost?

Get the necessary help to make the project/partnership a success.

1. Contact your state volunteer office (in Georgia 1-800-RingGBC)
2. Gather your materials.
3. Plan your budget.
4. Enlist your team.
5. Write your plan.

Train your team in the following areas:

1. Finances
2. Cultural information
3. Cross train each member using your materials
4. Evangelism
5. Personal follow-up

Go on your partnership trip and enjoy the time of your life.

CHAPTER 9

ACTS 1:8—MISSIONS EDUCATION

By Barbara Curnutt
Georgia WMU Executive Director-Treasurer

When a business in Washington, D.C. closed down, a sign on the front door read: GOING OUT OF BUSINESS. DIDN'T KNOW WHAT OUR BUSINESS WAS.

So, what is our business? Dr. W.O. Carver, revered Southern Baptist seminary professor in the early 1900s, used to begin each semester by asking his students, "What is the Bible all about? Or is it all about anything?"[1] Through the lectures that followed, Dr. Carver's students discovered the overall theme of the Bible. He helped them see the primary thread, the central theme that runs from Genesis to Revelation, revealing God's plan for world redemption.

God does have a plan, and it's our business! The center of His plan is Jesus Christ. The purpose of His plan is that all of the peoples of the earth may know and worship Him. And you and I, His church, are the instruments of this plan. We are called out and sent as His body into a lost and broken world. It begins and ends with God, but His eternal plan involves us. There's no room for spectators in God's plan, only participants. His plan, as described in Acts 1:8, is our business.

Somewhere very early in life, I learned that Jesus loves all the children of the world, and that we are called to share His love with the whole world. As a child involved in the missions organizations, I learned that I needed to know about the world, its people, and God's plan for the world. My lifelong journey through the missions organizations has made the difference

80

today in the way I view and interpret world events, in the way I pray and share my resources, and in the way I prioritize my life as an adult.

I am grateful for a wonderful missions leader who provided leadership and guidance for a rowdy, fun-loving group of children. Her life, her leadership and her compassion for a lost and hurting world greatly influenced who I am today. Sure, we had fun, but our leader invested her life in us week after week, as we participated in ministry projects and vicariously traveled the world together.

During those early years of heightened self-centeredness, we were presented the Acts 1:8 challenge and learned to turn our focus from ourselves to others. We began to see a world much bigger than the world we knew, a world for which Christ died. Without reservation, I know that my missions commitment was shaped in those formative and impressionable years because of consistent missions education opportunities.

As I reflect on my own experience, I am reminded of the words of Gaines Dobbins, respected Southern Baptist educator, who believed that the future of our missionary enterprise depends largely upon our effectiveness in enlisting and instructing the children and youth of each generation. He contended that it would be shortsighted to make our appeals only to adults because children and youth have limited resources and their interest is insignificant. It was Dr. Dobbins who also said, "If we fail to be missionary, we shall fail. In very truth the mission of the church is missions."[2]

Southern Baptists have always been known as a missions-motivated people. And yet, in the book, *Biblical Basis of Missions*, Avery Willis says, "Modern missions is the fad of a few. Not since the first century has missions been given its rightful place in the ministry of the church."[3] Even today only a small percentage of Southern Baptists have accepted the Acts 1:8 challenge and become involved in ongoing missions education.

How would you describe the missions health of your church? Do you have an Acts 1:8 strategy that enables all church members to understand and become involved in the mission of God? Are you intentional about educating the young, equipping and engaging the mature, and calling out the called? How well is your church doing in these areas: praying for and giving to missions, doing missions, learning about missions, and developing spiritually toward a missions lifestyle?

The truth is that a church is less likely to produce missions pray-ers, givers, or volunteers without an ongoing plan of nurture and encouragement. Rarely does one see young people or adults called of God into missions service out of a church that is indifferent toward missions.

Missions education is the responsibility of the church. "Missions" does not belong to Woman's Missionary Union, Men's Ministry, the International Mission Board or the North American Mission Board. It belongs to the church. Missionaries are not created or produced by mission boards and support organizations. Above all, they are called and gifted by God for the task, but they are taught, nurtured and sent out from the church. Those who will take the Gospel to the ends of the earth, as well as those who will stand in the gap providing support are in our churches today.

As we consider the future of missions, we must ask, "Who will be the ones who will go? Who will be the ones who pray? Who will be the ones to give of their financial resources in order to support our missions efforts?" These questions will not be resolved in a vacuum. If we neglect missions education today, the influence and impact of the church will be greatly diminished tomorrow. We must renew our commitment to invest intentionally and creatively in our preschoolers, children, youth and adults if we want to be significantly involved in what God is doing around the world.

We live in a world that is changing radically. Generational differences have impacted our churches with differing perspectives and needs. The influx of church members with no Southern Baptist background has offered new challenges and opportunities for church leaders. So how does the church fulfill its missions mandate in the midst of so many changes?

The church can recapture its responsibility for missions by:
- seeking God's vision through prayer and study of Scripture,
- developing healthy believers who are responsive to the eternal purposes of God,
- modeling and encouraging servanthood,
- placing greater emphasis on the Biblical basis of missions,
- communicating God's missionary purpose with enthusiasm and creativity,
- nurturing preschoolers, children and youth through quality missions education,
- offering adults and youth multiple options for experiential, interactive missions involvement,
- providing short-term opportunities and building on those experiences,
- placing more emphasis on participation and less on passive involvement,
- creating avenues for meaningful prayer involvement,
- calling out the called.

As world events unfold before our eyes, we are reminded of the impelling words of our Lord as recorded in Acts 1:8. Some have observed that not since the first century has the world been in greater tumult, nor have people been more responsive to the Gospel of Jesus Christ. What eternal difference is your church making in the community and around the world? Are you fostering an environment for children, youth, and adults to hear and respond to God's call to GO?

We stand at a crossroads today. There is an urgency about our missions mandate from which we cannot escape. We understand God's heart for the nations and His plan for world redemption. We realize that He has commissioned His Church to be His hands, His feet and His voice in carrying out that plan. And we know that we have little time to waste.

For information on available resources, contact Woman's Missionary Union and/or Men's Ministry of the Georgia Baptist Convention at 1-800-746-4422.

Endnotes

1. Winston Crawley, *Biblical Light for the Global Task*, p.10
2. Gaines S. Dobbins, *The Churchbook,* p. 227
3. Avery Willis, Jr., *Biblical Basis of Missions,* p.9

Bibliography:

Crawley, Winston. *Biblical Light for the Global Task.* Nashville, TN: Convention Press, 1978

Dobbins, Gaines S. *The Churchbook.* Nashville, TN: Broadman Press, 1951

Willis, Jr., Avery. *The Biblical Basis of Missions.* Nashville, TN: Convention Press, 1979

CHAPTER 10

ACTS 1:8 EVANGELISM STRATEGY
FROM
EVANGELISM MINISTRIES OF
THE GEORGIA BAPTIST CONVENTION

As we consider a Biblical evangelism strategy, we need to understand one issue critical to that strategy. When Jesus spoke to His disciples as recorded in Acts 1:8 and shared the divine evangelism strategy, He pointed out that His strategy is predicated upon the divine evangelism impulse and empowerment produced by the Holy Spirit. Evangelism is prompted by the Holy Spirit and empowers the Christian to be capable of carrying out the bold strategy Jesus shared. Jesus told His disciples that the Holy Spirit would prompt and empower a witnessing enterprise that would reach across the street and around the world! One cannot begin to create a strategy without taking a moment consider this issue.

Without the power of the Holy Spirit, we cannot enact the Acts 1:8 evangelism strategy presented by our Lord. Many Christians fail to be effective witnesses for Christ because they view the work of evangelism as reserved for a called-out minority or the talented few. Nothing could be further from the truth. Evangelism is the work of the Spirit of God through every believer who is obedient and submissive to the plan of God for reaching the world with the Gospel of Christ. A Biblical evangelism strategy must begin with this conviction.

Sadly, many believers do not accept the divine mandate found in Acts 1:8. No strategy that omits the Holy Spirit's empowerment for evangelism will ever be successful. In fact, it is the omission of Spiritual power for witnessing that has created the notion that most

Christians are exempt from witnessing. This false concept has resulted in a drop in baptisms across our Southern Baptist Convention that both puzzles and frightens our leaders. Consider the following statistics that are taken from the Annual Church Profiles of our churches across America. If we are baptizing people today at a resident member/baptism rate equal to that in 1950, Southern Baptists would have baptized over 800,000 people in 2002. But, how many did we baptize? The total baptisms in 2002 were less than 400,000. In other words, we are less than half as effective as those who served in our churches 50 years ago. Yet, we have modern equipment, better-trained leaders, and more beautiful church facilities by far than did our predecessors. In fact, if we continue to see our baptism ratio drop at the rate it has in recent years, by 2025, more than 70% of our churches will be baptizing 5 or less people per year all across our Southern Baptist Convention. this is disturbing and should sound an alarm!

We must go back to Acts 1:8 and implement a strategy based on God's **power**, God's **promise**, and God's **plan**! We need a revival of Spiritual fullness and a renewal to evangelistic effectiveness. Let me suggest several ways that we can move from stagnate evangelistic malaise to a recovery of spiritual evangelistic fervor.

The Power for the
Acts 1:8 Evangelism Strategy

Recognize the Power

The Lord told his disciples that He would provide the power for evangelism to a lost world. Note that He said, "You," shall receive power. To whom was Jesus speaking? He was addressing the New Testament Church and all who would become part of it in history. He was not speaking merely to the vocational ministers. He was not addressing the Roman government. He was not instructing the people who would teach in religious schools or seminaries. He was speaking to people like you and me. The reason many believers do not make themselves available as a witness for Christ is that they do not recognize that the power of the Holy Spirit already exists within them to assist in the ministry of evangelism. Until Christians fully recognize their dependence upon the Spirit of God for witnessing and the avail-ability of this power within them, they will never fulfill the Acts 1:8 Evangelism Strategy.

The power for carrying out an Acts 1:8 Evangelism Strategy is not merely denominational, personal, or organizational, it is SUPERNATURAL! That was the point Jesus was making to His disciples. Unless we know this fact and absorb it completely, we will never make ourselves available for the Lord's use in the min-istry of evangelism. After all, this was the Master's purpose when He was on the earth (Luke 19:10). If we follow in His footsteps, we will have the same purpose. But the purpose is not practical without the power.

The Spirit of the Lord was upon Christ to empower Him for His ministry (Luke 4:18), and He has given us His Spirit to enable us to do the work of evangelism (Acts 1:8). The power God gives us through His Spirit if like that which raised Jesus from the dead (Ephesians 1:18- 23). We cannot honestly say that we are incapable of doing the work of evangelism if we have such power within us.

Let us begin our strategy where Christ began it in Acts 1:8, "and you shall receive power after the Holy Spirit comes upon you." Church leaders must create a strategy for Acts 1:8 evangel-ism that includes a return to Spiritual infilling.

Realize the Power

A problem for most Christians, where evangelism is the issue, is the mistake of living daily in our own strength rather than living in dependence upon His Spirit. James W. Moore says, "One of the greatest comedy acts in the history of show business was the beloved husband and wife team of George Burns and Gracie Allen. In real life, Gracie Allen was a bright, wise businesswoman, but she always played the part of a naive, off-the-wall personality, sweetly simple in her approach to life. On one of their radio programs, Gracie became very upset because her new electric clock kept losing time. Each day it lost lots of time, so she finally called a repairman. He discovered the problem immediately. There was nothing wrong with the clock—it just wasn't plugged in! When George asked Gracie why it was unplugged, she said, "Well, I only need it when I need to know what time it is and I decided to turn it off in between to save electricity." I am afraid that is what many Christians attempt to do when it comes to the power of the Holy Spirit. We live in our own strength so much of the time that when we are required to do something (like witness to a lost person) that necessitates supernatural power, we find that we are lacking and unready. The power to witness is often missing because we fail to depend upon God's Spirit.

A do-it-yourselfer went into a hardware store early one morning and asked for a saw. The salesman took a chainsaw from the shelf and commented that it was the newest model, with the latest technology, and guaranteed to cut ten cords of wood a day. The customer thought that sounded pretty good, so he bought it on the spot. The next day the customer returned, looking somewhat exhausted.

"Something must be wrong with this saw," he moaned. "I worked as hard as I could and only managed to cut three cords of wood. I used to do four with my old-fashioned saw." Looking confused, the salesman said, "Here, let me try it out back on some wood we keep there." They went out to the woodpile, the salesman pulled the cord, and the motor went "Vvroooommmm!" The customer leaped back and exclaimed, "What's that noise!?"

Apparently the poor man had been cutting wood with a chain saw but had failed to start the motor. We must realize that the power to do God's work is found through the Spirit of the Lord. We must do our part, but doing our part without God's power is like trying to cut wood with a chainsaw that is not running!

Receive The Power

It is important to realize that we receive the power of God; we do not produce it! Jesus said in Acts 1:8, "And you shall receive power..." The power of God's Spirit is in every believer; however, it is possible for us to grieve or quench the Spirit and, thereby, to keep His power from working freely in and through us. Ephesians 4:29-32 reminds us that we grieve the Holy Spirit when our words and/or attitude are out of line with God's will. Many people cannot witness effectively because their attitudes and speech are totally incompatible with the nature of the Holy Spirit!

Many years ago, Dwight L. Moody was being used of God to touch the entire world. Several preachers were talking one day about the great work God was doing through Mr. Moody. One preacher was rather jealous of Moody and spoke up sarcastically saying, "Well, we should all remember that Dwight L. Moody does not have a monopoly on the Holy Spirit." One of the preachers in the conversation replied, "You are correct when you say that Dwight L. Moody does not have a monopoly on the Holy Spirit, but I perceive that the Holy Spirit has a monopoly on Dwight L. Moody." We must allow God's Spirit to take control of our attitudes and words! It is a sin to fail in our witnessing, but it is preceded by the sin of having a heart that is not totally yielded to the Lord and, therefore, a heart not filled with God's Spirit.

Also, we may quench the Holy Spirit by putting out the fire that the Spirit desires to build in our hearts for evangelism (1 Thessalonians 5:19). How does one put out a fire? When you place anything on a fire that is not combustible, you begin to quench the fire. Putting out the Holy Spirit's fire for evangelism is no different. We may have events at our churches that are for good purposes, but unless we build into them an evangelistic strategy, we are throwing water on the Spirit's fire for evangelism. A fire without something combustible will soon go out completely. Many churches have great programs but win few people to Christ. Why? They have quenched the Holy Spirit by leaving out the evangelism dimension. The events may go on but the church fails to reach people for Christ. The plans and programs of the church become internal! If you want a conflagration in your midst, make sure evangelism is included in everything you do at the local church level.

To summarize, we can say that a proper attitude prohibits grieving the Holy Spirit and that proper actions prohibit quenching the Holy Spirit. The correct attitude assists us in remaining pure vessels for the Holy Spirit to fill, and proper evangelistic action aligns us for the Spirit's fire to burn brightly through us.

An action may not be especially evil but still be very detrimental in our evangelistic effectiveness. Consider a person who is an incessant worrier. A lady goes to work and talks regularly with a co-worker about her worries. She is worried about finances, health and family issues. Then, one day, she decides to invite her co-worker to church. Can you imagine being her non-church attending co-worker? Would you want to go to church with her? The worried church attender has given out a message of fear, doubt and discouragement. The non-church attender has enough problems without going to church and ending up like the worried church lady! The Christian's attitude of worry and doubt can grieve the Spirit and quench the fire of evangelism.

An Acts 1:8 strategy for evangelism must emphasize a dependence upon the Holy Spirit backed by a life of proper attitudes and actions. Any strategy that begins with plans without first emphasizing the power will be faulty at best and a disaster at worst.

As part of your Acts 1:8 strategy, be sure to take the following steps. Also, if you are pastor, lead your church to do likewise. Perhaps a sermon, series of sermons, or a Bible study could be used to bring the congregation to a point of renewed commitment to the Holy Spirit. Remember that a plan without power will be pathetic! But a strategic plan, coupled with God's awesome power, will be potent!

- Ask God to forgive you for seeking to serve Him in your own power.
- Admit that you cannot be an effective witness without His power.
- Ask Him to reveal obstructions to the Spirit's power in your life.
- As they are revealed repent of the attitudes and actions that block the spirit.

- Affirm your responsibility and willingness to be empowered to witness.
- Ask God to give you someone to witness to DAILY.
- Apply these principles to a strategy for Acts 1:8 Evangelism in your church.

The Promise for the Acts 1:8 Evangelism Stragegy

God has PROMISED to empower us to witness. God never made a promise that He did not keep; nor has He ever made a promise that He will not keep. The promise God made regarding being His witnesses needs to be clarified somewhat before we fully grasp the assurance of this specific promise.

The Promise was not for Conversions in Every Witnessing Experience

First, God did not promise that we would have converts to Christ each time we witness for Him. In the Scriptures we discover that Jesus warned His disciples that a witness for Him would bring about persecution (John 16:1-3). Every faithful witness for Christ is successful regardless of the results. Christ promised us power to witness, but the results of that witness is between God and the person who receives the witness.

The Promise was not for Comfort in our Witnessing Experience.

Second, God did not promise that witnessing would be easy. Some Christians find it difficult to witness and assume that they are just "not cut out to be evangelistic." This is a sad conclusion. Even many pastors find it difficult to witness, and some of the most effective lay witnesses within the kingdom still face witnessing with trepidation and hesitancy. A feeling of weakness in witnessing can, in fact, be of great assistance to you. Why? Because it casts you upon the mercy and grace of God. The power to witness is not in you, but rather it is from Him If we could do it without Him, we would not need the promise of Acts 1:8

The Promise was for being Obedient as a Witness

Third, the promise of Acts 1:8 is for the Spirit's power to assist us in sharing our love for Jesus with others no matter the consequences, fears or problems we may face. In a way, we can say that success in witnessing is not found in winning the lost, or being accepted by those to whom we witness, but in being lovingly faithful to share the Good News in whatever circumstances we find ourselves. God's power is given to us so we can do what He has called us to do no matter what kind of response we receive from the world.

The Promise was for doing the Impossible in being a Witness

Fourth, the promise of Acts 1:8 extends beyond a personal witness to a worldwide witness. It is difficult for us to imagine the promise of Acts 1:8 as it would have sounded to those who first heard the words. To that small band of believers gathered in Jerusalem, Jesus promised a witness to the entire world. How could that be possible? In an age without radios, televisions, satellites orbiting the earth, cell phones, or jet planes, how could a rag-tag group of uneducated men take a witness to the entire world? In essence, that was not a problem at all. Why? Because God promised HE would give them the POWER to carry out the command to go into all the world! God never tells His people to do something that He will not enable them to accomplish. **Capability** is **responsibility** matched with **availability!** If God gives me the responsibility, I will be capable if I am fully available and dependent upon His Spirit to empower me for evangelistic ministry.

The Plan for the Acts 1:8 Evangelism Strategy

We come now to the strategic portion of our look at the Acts 1:8 Evangelism Strategy. Our Lord communicated a plan for sharing the Good News with the entire world. The plan involves several facets. Before we look at four critical parts of the divine strategy, lets consider an important point.

The Acts 1:8 Evangelism Strategy is for every believer and every local church. Our Lord did not give this plan to an extraordinary group of people. Look at the experience of the woman at the well as recorded in the Gospel of John, Chapter 4. Jesus encountered a woman at the well outside the Samaritan village of Sychar. There are many lessons in this encounter, but I want us to focus on just one issue. Once this woman trusted Christ as the Savior, she went back to the city and shared a witness concerning Christ, the Messiah! Why is this so important to understanding Acts 1:8? Just this, the woman had been married five times and was living with a man to whom she was not married. She did not have the social credentials, educational credentials or moral credentials to make her a witness for Christ. She spent less than one hour talking with Jesus, so it is apparent that she could not have possibly received much in the way of theological training. Her conversation with Jesus revealed that in some ways she was a confused woman when it came to understanding the basics of faith and God's Word. Yet, because she believed in Christ, she ran back to the city and told what she had experienced. Her witness was not powerful because of her training. Her witness was not powerful because of her education. Her witness was not powerful because of her vocabulary. Her witness was not powerful because of her theological understanding. Her witness was not powerful because of her use of positive thinking or post-mortem psychology. Her witness WAS POWERFUL because she had been with JESUS!

Those of us who have received Jesus as Savior have His presence with us in the person of the Holy Spirit. He has promised us POWER to be His witnesses. No amount of earthly accomplishments, training, gifts or social contacts can make us effective witnesses. God's Spirit can use these things, but we must remember that the power of the Holy Spirit is the real need for effective evangelism.

That which is applied to the individual believer can also be applied to the local church. Each church is made up of believers; therefore, each church should have an Acts 1:8 Evangelism Strategy. This strategy should involve at least four components.

It must be a Verbal Strategy

A church cannot have a non-verbal strategy for obeying Acts 1:8. A witness must "tell" what has happened to Him. The disciples spoke when they witnessed, "For we cannot help speaking about what we have seen and heard" (Acts 4:20 NIV). A witness must "speak." A witness in a court case cannot testify to the truth or lack of truth in court just by the way he lives each day. How much more important it is for a believer to testify verbally concerning all that Christ has done and is doing for him or her.

The verbal strategy extends to ministries in the church and outside the church. In Sunday School, discipleship classes, training courses, sermons, and musical presentations, the people of God must share a verbal witness to the saving work of Christ.

Why is it necessary for a verbal witness to be shared? Because a verbal witness, using God's Word, is the plan God has chosen to use and to bless. The Scripture states it like this, "So then faith comes by hearing, and hearing by the word of God." (Romans 10:17 NKJV) People need to hear the Word of God, shared by a faithful witness who gives evidence to its truth, in order to have believing faith.

Witness Training is very important for assisting believers in sharing verbally their faith in Christ with others. We must never give the impression that training alone can produce an effective witness for Christ, but when a trained witness who is yielded to the Holy Spirit goes forth with faith and confidence, good things will happen.

In order to develop a strategy for verbal witnessing, the pastor must have a plan for emphasizing verbal witnessing, a plan for training personal witnessing, a plan for undergirding this witnessing ministry with prayer and a plan for actually doing the work of verbally witnessing in the local "Jerusalem."

Jesus said that the Holy Spirit would empower believers to be witnesses in Jerusalem, Judea, Samaria and the uttermost part of the earth. "Jerusalem" speaks of the area and community, city and county where we live. In other words, you cannot simply pay someone else to do your witnessing for you! You cannot fulfill the

Great Commission of Matthew 28: 18-20 or the Power Promise of Acts 1:8 by merely giving to and praying for missions., Though both giving to and praying for evangelism/missions are important, they do not take the place of a verbal witness for Christ.

Also, preaching is a large part of the verbal witness of the local church. Though many churches have given up on evangelistic services, sometimes called revivals, others are discovering afresh that revivals are a great way to reach lost and unchurched people. One church in the Georgia Baptist Convention recently held a revival with amazing results. The church is in a rural area, has had the same pastor for 14 years, and has an attendance of less than 100 per week. This is not the kind of church you would think of as producing an effective Acts 1:8 Strategy. But, this pastor decided he would use an old-fashioned revival as a means of sharing a verbal witness with the community. After attending training on how to prepare for revival services, the pastor set about to involve his entire church in the process of experiencing real revival. The church prepared for months. They prayed, promoted, witnessed and publicized the meeting. Prayerful consideration was given to the right evangelist to preach. In the end, the revival was held and 31 people were baptized into that church! Wow! That is truly amazing. Or is it? God promised that we would have power in our evangelism if we would trust His Holy Spirit to enable us to do what we cannot do alone! The church added revival planning to their strategy, worked hard to implement the plan, trusted God's Spirit to bless their efforts, and the results were wonderful!

The pastor of the local church, and each Sunday School teacher, should regularly tell people how to be saved. Some people are not saved because no one has told them what they are to do in order to receive God's gift of eternal life in Christ. We just assume all those present in our classes or worship services know how to be saved, or we assume that they are already saved. Yet, churches that regularly tell people how to be saved, and give them an opportunity to respond, share wonderful stories of God's salvation occurring in their services. Sometimes even church members who have not actually been converted accept Christ in those churches. Use the pulpit and the podium as part of your overall Acts 1:8 Evangelism Strategy.

It Must be a Personal Strategy

The fact that my evangelism strategy must be verbal means that it must also be personal. In other words, I must speak about something that is personal to me. Mark 5 contains the story of a man possessed with a legion of demons. This man met Jesus and was gloriously and miraculously delivered. Later, this delivered man asked Christ if he might go with Him on his journeys. Look at the plan Jesus presents to this man: "However, Jesus did not permit him, but said to him, 'Go home to your friends, and tell them what great things the Lord has done for you, and how He has had compassion on you.' And he departed and began to proclaim in Decapolis all that Jesus had done for him; and all marveled" (Mark 5:19-20 NKJV). The delivered man was told to go and tell what had been done for him by the Lord. We are to tell personally what Christ has done for us.

A personal strategy for Acts 1:8 evangelism will involve three personal elements:
- What my life was like before I met Christ
- How I came to trust Christ as my Savior and Lord
- What my life is like now that I know Christ personally

If I testify as I should, aided by the power of the Holy Spirit, it will naturally lead me to ask those to whom I speak, "Has anything like this happened to you?" That will open the door for me to share how any person can trust Christ, turn from sin, and be gloriously saved.

It stands to reason that a person cannot tell a personal story of salvation if he or she does not have such a story to tell. It is critical that every church member be truly saved. A lost church member may increase the numerical membership roll, add to the attendance records, and even give some funds for the church's ministry. But the lost church member has no salvation story to tell and cannot be a witness for Christ. The Holy Spirit does not indwell the lost church member, and because of this he or she will almost assuredly become a hindrance to the witness of the entire church.

New member classes and follow up visits are essential for those who make a decision for Christ and/or request membership in the local church. These are opportunities to ensure that every person who joins is actually saved.

On occasion a redeemed church member will publicly do something that is a bad witness for Christ and His Church. For this reason, church discipline must be used as a means of revealing to members and the community that such behavior is not appropriate. This is not to say that church discipline should be harsh or punishing. Indeed, the purpose of church discipline is to restore a believer completely to the service and joy of the Lord. Nonetheless, the church must not wink at sin and look the other way when open sin is being practiced by church members. This kind of complicity in sinful behavior sends an inappropriate message to the community and can result in God's power being removed from that fellowship for years to come!

It Must Be a Global Strategy

An Acts 1:8 Church Evangelism Strategy will have a global aspect. Jesus told the disciples that the witness He empowered would reach to the ends of the earth. The disciples did not ask how this was to be done, though surely they must have wondered. Today, we see the methods God is using to bring His message of love and salvation to all people. We must not become complacent in this technologically advanced age. Technology is not the answer to reaching the world—it is merely a tool. The people of the world must be reached by redeemed, obedient, witnessing people.

A global strategy for evangelism involves several aspects. First prayer is essential. We need a prayer ministry in our local churches that reveals our trust in God, our compassion for a lost world, and our dependence upon God's Spirit in order to carry out a worldwide evangelism ministry.

Second, we must give faithfully to mission causes. The cost of doing evangelistic work in over 100 countries around the world is awesome. Certainly, no one family, one church, one state convention or group can meet the need alone. Each believer and each church must do their best to meet the challenges of reaching our world with the Gospel of Christ. Materialism and hedonism are dangerous traps for the modern Christian. We must reject the "keeping up with the Joneses" syndrome that plagues so much of our society. Churches must clearly present the missionary and evangelism needs of the world to their congregations so members can develop a heart of compassion and a strategy of stewardship that will honor the Lord. The believer must not be allowed to think that evangelism stops at the church door or at the city limit sign!

Third, personal involvement in evangelistic journeys must be encouraged. To travel outside of America to share Jesus is a humbling and astounding experience. Those who make such trips often become the most effective evangelism leaders in the local church once they return. Why? Because they have seen how blessed we are here in America. Also, they have faced their fears about witnessing and have discovered the joy of overcoming that fear. Lastly, they cast themselves in full trust upon the Holy Spirit to empower them. In essence, they have become Acts 1:8 Christians.

Each church should seek to be involved in mission trips that encompass personal witnessing. These trips can be within one's state, somewhere in America and/or trips overseas. Some churches are not large enough to arrange such trips, but even the smallest churches can arrange to have one or more of their members join a mission trip arranged through the association, state convention, or national mission's agency.

Summary of Strategies for Acts 1:8 Evangelism
- Preach a series of sermons of God's Power for evangelistic ministry calling believers to a commitment, not a commitment to evangelism, but primarily a commitment

to trust the power of the Holy Spirit to enable them to be evangelistic
- Teach a discipleship course on the work of the Holy Spirit in witnessing
- Solemn Assembly
- Include confession of sin in every Wednesday prayer meeting
- Make books and literature available to members on personal evangelism, prayer, spiritual awakening, and the Holy Spirit
- Identify opportunities to witness each day of the week
- Identify opportunities for evangelism in every church ministry and activity
- Train church members to start conversations with strangers
- Train church members how to witness specifically to family members and friends
- Identify how church members can verbalize the gospel in
  - Jerusalem
  - Judea
  - Samaria
  - Ends of the Earth
- Lead the church in a study of church discipline
- Training members to use all means of witnessing, including
  - Testimony
  - Tracts
  - Marked New Testament
- Identify association and state convention opportunities for training and mission trips.

Presented by:
Evangelism Ministries, Georgia Baptist Convention

CHAPTER 11

The Acts 1:8 Challenge: Church Planting For Rapid Multiplication

Reproducing Healthy Kingdom Churches that Empower Kingdom Growth

I will begin this chapter with a story. Recently one of my colleagues was on his way to church with his family. His seven- year old daughter looked out the car window and saw a man working in his yard. She said, "Daddy, that man needs to go in and get ready for church." Dad agreed and responded, "There are millions of people who don't attend church on Sunday." She paused for a moment and exclaimed, "Dad, we need more churches for these people." I have pondered that statement from this young seven-year old for quite some time. Why didn't she say, "He needs to come to our church." Or what about, "We need to invite him to our church." My speculation is that this young millennial hasn't been thoroughly encoded with the boomer culture that would suggest that her church could reach everyone in the area. To be sure, her church might be effective in reaching this unchurched gentleman. However, it may take another new church with a new approach to reach him.

Introduction

Church planting is the most effective strategy the early apostles used effectively to win the known world to Christ.[1] These multiplying, healthy planted churches turned the world upside down with the message of Jesus. The Book of Acts is actually a history of church planting that records God's intentional missional acts of planting churches of every people group and culture in the known world at that time. However, it is far more than history. Today it serves the missional evangelical church as the best "how to" church planting manual in print. This chapter is written with the vision and belief that this same Jesus wants to do it again. His preferred vision is a rapid multiplication of healthy kingdom churches. Dr. J. Robert White wrote, "The truth of the matter is, every congregation can participate in church multiplication."[2]

The pattern for rapid multiplication of churches is found in the New Testament. God has a preferred future for the world and is orchestrating a church planting movement to fulfill His mission. He continues to invite us to join him. Acts 1:8 is about reducing lost populations by bringing them to Christ. It is about penetrating the darkness and transforming communities. In this chapter the reader will review the visionary and intentional steps a church may take to fulfill an Acts 1:8 church planting strategy. These four steps are

Step 1: Discover God's Church Planting Vision
Step 2: Develop God's Church Planting Strategy
Step 3: Establish Goals and Organize Church for Extension
       Growth
Step 4: Prioritize Plans, Calendar, Budget to Reach Acts 1:8
       Goals

Step 1:
Discover God's Church Planting Vision

The church must discover God's vision and mandate of reaching all people everywhere. Other chapters have emphasized other important missional perspectives of an Acts 1:8 church, but it might be helpful to ask the question: When Jesus first told the disciples to go everywhere to reach everyone, did they understand to be witnesses meant to go grow their church or did they understand that it meant to go reach people and assimilate them into multiple communities of faith? The answer to the question is obvious. However, many North American churches have lost sight of our Lord's original intention of Acts 1:8 and adopted a church growth mentality based more on corporate America than the Bible. For the most part, marginal North American churches define success as anything bigger-namely budgets, baptisms, buildings as the criteria for gauging health and success. Don't misunderstand, it's important for churches to grow, but what about growing bigger, and better, and broader?[3] The Acts 1:8 church must reexamine the Biblical model of growth and reestablish the priority of reaching all people.

The Biblical model of church growth is one of expansion and extension (and bridging).[4] The early church ultimately reached throughout Asia Minor. It is not the purpose of this chapter to do a thorough study of church growth. The reader is encouraged to read through the *Book of Acts* and Donald McGavran's definitive work, *Understanding Church Growth.* Suffice it to say that the bulk of church growth material since McGavran has focused on the expansion, that is the numerical aspects, of "growing the church" rather than the other half of his study which deals with extension church planting. Why is this so important?

Our Culture. The predominant culture in the last quarter of the twentieth century was a boomer culture. It continued to be shaped by the industrial revolution. This boomer and industrial culture has helped shape our understanding of church and church success in America. "Bigger" has always meant better. As a young church planter in the 80's, I knew full well what guests and new members were expecting from the new church. They expected bigger and better programs and facilities than the church down the street! They demanded resources to meet their needs as religious consumers! Our industrial mindset set the stage to build an institution through more baptisms, bigger buildings, and budgets.

Our Church Culture. I also knew full well what my colleagues were asking when they asked at the Monday morning pastor's conference, "How did Sunday go?" It was their way of asking, "How was attendance?," "How was the offering?," "How is the building program?," "Who and how many joined?" Here is where the difficulty comes into focus. A church's success in the 20th century began to be defined as increased numerical growth. To be sure these are important questions and the church that is healthy is a growing church! But, real growth is bigger than that! Real growth is measured by multiplying disciples and churches. There was no real discussion about kingdom growth and multiplying churches at Associational Pastor Conferences that I attended in the 80's.

The "mega" church has contextualized well in our boomer and industrial culture. However, for the most part, much of our success has continued to be defined in quantitative ways. As church success began to be defined exclusively as increased numerical growth, the pastor who had led the church with more baptisms, larger buildings, and bigger budgets had a much better probability of being recognized as successful. Our boomer church culture has had no problem accepting half of the church growth understanding of the New Testament. It's almost like we read **half of** the book of Acts and **half** of McGavran's definitive work on church growth.

To be sure the church has had tremendous impact in the world through the many baptisms, bigger buildings and programs, and larger budgets to provide resources. There is no question in my mind that God has used the contextualization of the mega church in a "bigger is better" culture to reach boomers who were looking at the church as a resourceful institution. This has been and will continue to be a tremendous way of reaching people. But, again, true success is broader. The Acts 1:8 Challenge is to rediscover rapid multiplication.

The New Testament church extended herself through reproduction and multiplication of churches. It's the other **half** of the church growth equation that presents for us a challenge as we move into the 21st century. As already referenced, to use McGavran's terminology, the New Testament pattern is expansion and extension. **The "mega" church of the 20th century, as well as other churches, must become the "multiplying" church of the 21st century in order to be faithful to the New Testament definition of church growth and reach masses of unchurched people.**

In the New Testament it is clear that God called and gifted church planters. The apostles were church planting missionaries and planted new churches to not only expand but to extend the kingdom of God throughout Asia Minor and the rest of the world. The New Testament church expanded through extension growth! The goal of the New Testament church was to reach people, The Acts 1:8 Strategy focuses on going everywhere while Matthew 28 Strategy focuses on reaching everyone!

In order to reach the world the church must continue to emphasize the calling of this apostolic church planting gift in the body of Christ. These missionary pioneers should be enlisted, encouraged, equipped, and empowered to start new ministries and new work. Just as the church celebrates the call of international and domestic missionaries they need to begin celebrating the call in the lives of those called to start new ministries and new work to reach unreached people groups in their own Jerusalem, Judea, and...(Acts1:8).

Our Denominational Culture. More churches are parenting new work. Many churches are partnering with other churches to start new churches. Denominations and Associations are connecting together to assist new churches and parent churches. Networks are forming as churches cluster together to begin new work together.

A major component of the movement is the Minister of Missions movement.* Many Acts 1:8 churches continue to add additional staffing and budget resources to reach people. The Minister of Missions implements the mission vision of the local church to reach the world. This new emphasis on missions is fueling the emphasis on reproduction and multiplication on the local level as well as overseas. (*See *Appendixes* for information concerning Acts 1:8 Key Churches.)

Postmodernity will change the face of our modern culture as well as have a tremendous impact on our church culture. Negatively, the postmodern emphasis on pluralism and relativism will continue to challenge the church. Though there is always negative impact when culture transforms church rather than the church transforming culture, the upcoming postmodern culture will impact the church in a healthy way as more and more Christian "post moderns" desire to "experience" missions. The church "busters" will be more personally involved in missions and church planting. The younger "millenial" members will desire to personally "participate" in church planting. **Denominational agencies will no longer do missions on behalf of the church, but will resource the church to carry out her understanding of mission in a local and global context.** Our understanding of "Healthy Growth" will undergo a major redefining. Healthy kingdom churches will intentionally plant churches.[5]

Our Current Church Growth Culture. The modern church growth movement has served the "boomerized" church well, but has not kept the challenge of extension growth before us. The emphasis on numerical growth has produced a church culture where less than 2-3% of our churches are involved in church planting to any degree other than giving through the denominational agency. (In the 20th Century paradigm the agencies did mission on behalf of the member churches.) The 20th century church did extension growth through giving financial resources to mission boards rather than through personal commitment and involvement. This served a boomerized church culture well with emphasis on institutional growth and numerical church growth. The modern church growth movement is short sighted and doesn't carry growth far enough. The Healthy 21st Century Church will move beyond church growth with a clear focus on kingdom growth. It must have God's vision for kingdom advancement as well as a Biblical strategy to fulfill the vision.

Step 2:
Develop God's Church Planting Strategy

The New Testament pattern of doing ministry and starting churches begins with a clear focus on people and people groups.[6] Biblical, incarnational ministry implies going where the people are in order to win them to Christ. Servant evangelism and relational evangelism imply finding people where they are, meeting their needs in the name of Jesus (without insisting that they help expand a particular local church), and clearly sharing the gospel. After successful evangelism, in the New Testament, the households where congregationalized into new churches and rapidly began reaching new people groups.[7] Nate Adams explains, "When the gospel is successfully planted, new churches grow and multiply."[8] He goes on to say,

> "The unchanging gospel speaks to diverse cultures and generations through new leaders and new methods in new churches. As cultural pioneers and creative missionaries establish relationships and evangelize in North America, today's churches also need to be ready with strategies for establishing relevant new churches and preparing capable new leaders. Many of these new strategies will be very different from those of their partner churches, because they will be designed to make disciples in a different cultural context."[9]

As Len Sweet reminds us, the church can no longer remain under the steeple and yell to the neighborhood, "be here."[10] To the contrary, the church must "be there" in extension ministry, extension evangelism, and extension church growth. Much of our postmodern and post-Christian culture no longer looks favorably at the "institutional" church. Agnostic and ignostic persons will not come to the church for church programs to help the church grow. They are lost without Christ and understandably indifferent toward the church. **The church must extend herself into the community**

106

in order to reach those who have "cocooned" themselves into their own isolated communities and sub-cultures. **Evangelism must be the heartbeat of every ministry! Congregationalizing is a natural by-product of evangelism when the assimilation process requires developing indigenous leadership to reach new language, social-economic, cultural, or generational people groups.** The new church will rapidly reach the new people group when social and cultural barriers are broken down and overcome through relationships and networking.

The Acts 1:8 healthy kingdom church will deal with *spiritual pride.* The significant church of the 21st will long longer be satisfied with announcing church activities and ministries and expect people to come just because the doors are open. The healthy church will take initiative to do ministry outside the four walls of the church. The "be here" mentality that worked in a friendly culture will be transformed into a "be there" mentality to reach people who no longer respond to church activities inside the building and institution. The healthy church will do ministry where the people are!

The Acts 1:8 healthy kingdom church will deal with *social prejudice.* The significant church of the 21st century will reach out to all people everywhere regardless of sinful background, racial identity, socio-economic status. Reaching red, yellow, black, and white will be much more than a song, it will be heartfelt conviction informed by divine mandate. In the new vision, multiple churches will be started of all kinds of *ethnos.*

The healthy kingdom church will deal with *special cultural preferences.* The significant church of the 21st century will not allow yesterday's cultural preferences to hinder the practice of Biblical functions of the church in new cultural forms. New, relevant forms will be preferred in order to reach masses of unchurched people. The healthy church will become "all things to all people" to reach as many lost as possible. The content of the contextual message and ministry must be determined by a uncompromising commitment to the Bible; the cultural form must be determined by an unapologetic commitment to reach people for whom Christ died in a language and culture that can be understood. Empowered and enabled by the Spirit of God, the balance of doing ministry and sharing the message of Christ between these "two worlds" will ultimately determine the fruitfulness and effectiveness of reaching new communities and people groups who need Jesus.

For effective church planting and extension ministries the church must direct her energy as well as her resources to the Acts 1:8 communities. The role of the church in the community is clearly that of a servant. Personnel and finances must be budgeted for Acts 1:8 community ministries. Effective ministry will be in the streets, at the park and in the community center or theater. The modern day Lydias (Acts 16) will be found outside the church. To be certain the church will continue to expand, however, the church must without apology commit to extend herself into the communities in order to reach the lost and diverse neighborhoods. In order to reach the world the church must continue to emphasize the apostolic gift in the body of Christ. These "pioneer" missionaries should be enlisted, encouraged, equipped, and empowered to start new ministries and new work around the globe through networking and partnerships.

The Acts 1:8 Church will be committed to direct and indirect missions and church planting. They will be personally involved in church planting around the world. They will reestablish missional goals and reorganize to meet those goals.

Step 3:
Establish Goals and Organize For Extension Growth

After discovering vision and developing strategy, the church must establish church planting goals and organize to fulfill their mission. These goals should center around an Acts 1:8 vision and strategy. The church should consider the following:

1. Adopt a Church Wide Mission Statement. Many churches do this. Every church should have a clear and articulated mission statement that is published and promoted regularly. Casting the vision of church planting must be central to the comprehensive strategy to effectively reach people.

2. Realize the magnitude of the vision and call a Minister of Missions. Many churches take this next step. The Acts 1:8 strategy requires personnel. Every church needs a church planting point person. This person can be full-time, part-time, or a volunteer. In order to keep the focus of Acts 1:8, the MOM must recruit and train a point person for each dimension of Acts 1:8.[11]

3. Develop and train the OnMission Team. The OnMission Team needs at least four point persons. Each of these persons should enlist and train a team committed to one of the Acts 1:8 emphases. They should work together with the MOM and other staff to coordinate the mission calendar and budget. The four subteams are built around the Acts 1:8:

   1) Jerusalem: Local Missions and Ministries
   2) Judea: Associational and State Partners
   3) Samaria: NAMB Partnerships-Mission
   4) Uttermost: IMB Partnerships

   The effective Acts 1:8 Church will **reestablish goals and reorganize** in order to provide intentional leadership in all four areas of Acts 1:8. Point persons will be called out with passion. They will be given monies in the church budget as well as priority calendar space to fulfill the mission.

4. Commit to the on going mission education of the church by enculturating the mission education curriculum with church planting strategy and goals.[12]

5. Prioritize mission involvement to include calling out the members to help with church plants and creating partnerships of new work on the associational, state, national, and international levels.)

Step 4:
Prioritize Plans, Calendar, Budget to Reach Acts 1:8 Goals

I close with one more story. Robin came to her first Bible Study because of a personal invitation of a recently saved neighbor, Gloria. Just a few days before, Gloria had been saved by accepting Christ through a door-to-door survey and had agreed to host the Bible study in her home. During the simple reading of the third chapter of the Gospel of John, Robin indicated she wanted to be "born again" by asking, "does this mean I can be born again tonight?" Robin and several of her friends found new life in Christ that evening and a new church was born as an extension of a parent church. It is very unlikely that Robin and her neighborhood friends would have ever attended an established local church. She was "cocooned" in her community and very isolated from the local churches other than an occasional summer activity.

What does Robin's conversion tell us about being the multiplying church in the 21st century? How do we reach the millions of Robins and Glorias in new communities? **The church must reexamine the biblical model of extension church growth, reestablish the priority of reaching people, and redirect her energies and resources to off campus ministries and new starts. The effectiveness of this "kingdom growth movement" will be determined by the church's commitment to the extension growth of the church.**

Long range plans for the Acts 1:8 Church will take a "broader" approach than before. Unsatisfied with just growing one church in a dominant culture, the Acts 1:8 Church will make decisive plans to start new ministries and churches looking at 5, 10, and even 15 to 20 years out.

Calendaring for the Acts 1:8 Challenge Church will include making room in the weekly and yearly schedule for significant mission processes and events. Priority to mission education and mission involvement will be evidenced by the overall calendar. The Acts 1:8 challenge church will coordinate On Mission Celebrations, Commissioning services, mission training and events with the overall calendaring of the church.

Budgets are vision and mission statements. They speak to the values in the church. Increased budgets for mission endeavors will range from supporting mission education, mission partnerships, and church planting as line items in the mission budget. The conscientious mission minded and kingdom focused church will incrementally increase the Cooperative Program, State Missions, and Association amount or percentages to align with the missionary vision of the church and the Acts 1:8 Strategy.

Many experts suggest we are in a major transition as we move through postmodernity.[14] Strategic praying and thinking will continue to be necessary as the church and denomination deal with cultural change in order to achieve excellence and maximize effectiveness. Our thinking must be informed by Biblical mandate and cultural relevancy in order to be contextualized to the predominate cultures to reach the most people through indigenous evangelism and church planting.

It is an exciting day for churches and denominations when God has led them to partner together to reach people through the multiplying of Healthy Kingdom Churches. Healthy Kingdom Churches will continue to cooperate together in order to reach the most people for Christ.

Endnotes

1 Peter Wagner, *Church Planting For a Greater Harvest: A Comprehensive Guide,* (Regal Books: Ventura, CA 1982), Introduction.

2 See J. Robert White, *Healthy Kingdom Churches: Ten Qualities of Healthy Churches* (Baptist Press: Friendswood, TX, 2002). Chapter 5 of this book is given to the vision of multiplication.

3 Ebbie Gibbs, *Growing Healthy Churches*

4 See Donald McGavrans' definitive books on church growth, *Understanding Church Growth* and *The Bridges of God.*

5 See Ed Stetzer, Church *Planting In a Postmodern* Age (Lifeway: Nashville, TN, 2003).

6 Acts

7 Acts 16

8 Nate Adams, *The Acts 1:8 Challenge: Empowering the Church to Be On Mission* (Lifeway Press: Nashville, TN, 2004)

9 Ibid, *The Acts 1:8 Challenge*

10 Len Sweet, *Postmodern Pilgrims*

11 See Appendix

12 A good example of this would be using Nate Adams' *The Acts 1:8 Challenge* book. It is the 2005 doctrinal study.

13 See chapter 8. See contact your association, state, NAMB, and IMB partnership opportunity.

14 Acts 1:8 churches must think missionally long range.

Glossary of Terms for Church Planting

millennial–the younger generation from around 2000

missional–mission-minded, on mission

contextualized–putting the message in a way that communicates with cultures

apostolic–missionary-like

post modernity–the philosophy and world view after the modern time

pluralism–all philosophies are equally valid

relativeism–no absolute truth

busters–generation born between 1950-2000

paradigm–a mental model or a new way of thinking

incarnational–cross-cultural missions that result in cultural expressions of truth

agnostic–someone who is not sure about spiritual beliefs

ignostic–someone who does not know

indigenous–a native of a specific area or culture

ethnos–ethnic group, people group

enculturating–engaging the target culture

APPENDIX

ACTS 1:8 STRATEGY

I. Take the HKC diagnostic

II. An Acts 1:8 strategy is a strategy that makes missions/evangelism a priority through a balanced and consistent effort to reach my Jerusalem, my Judea, my Samaria, and the uttermost parts of the world, under the empowerment of the Holy Spirit.
    A. Acts 1:8 sets missions/evangelism as a priority in:
        1. Budget
        2. Prayer
        3. Time
        4. Programs
        5. Education
    B. Acts 1:8 sets a balance in the four primary ministry fields: home, state, country, and world.

        In light of this definition, assess your current reality.
        1. Am I an Acts 1:8 individual?
        2. Is my church an Acts 1:8 church?
        List in two columns the information you use to determine your current reality:
                Column I (yes) Column II (no)

III. Strategy questions
     Do I want to be an Acts 1:8 person and be a part of an Acts 1:8 church? Why, or why not?

IV. Acts 1:8 strategy for an individual, church, or association:
    Resources needed:
    A. Facilitator.
    B. Acts 1:8 Strategy book by Dr. Mike Gravette
        1. A trained facilitator will meet with a church to give an overview of the Acts 1:8 strategy material from *Acts 1:8 Strategy.*

2. The church can invite the facilitator to lead the study for the church.
3. It will take 10 hours to complete the material.
4. Each individual will sign an Acts 1:8 covenant.
5. The church will vote to covenant to become an Acts 1:8 church and post the covenant promise.
6. The church will plan the four-phase mission outreach effort.
7. The church will sign up on the Georgia Baptist Convention/NAMB web site as an Acts 1:8 church.
8. The church will commit to promoting the church as a Mission/Evangelism church in:

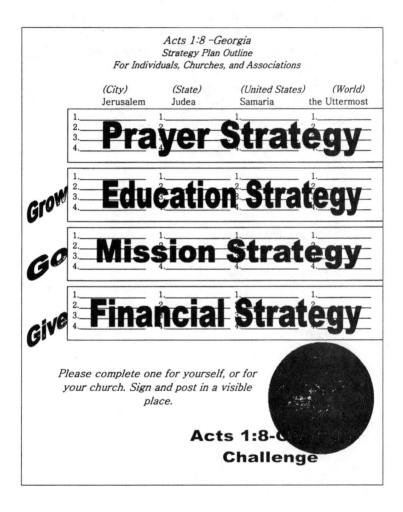

Acts 1:8 –Georgia
Strategy Plan Outline
For Individuals, Churches, and Associations

(City)	(State)	(United States)	(World)
Jerusalem	Judea	Samaria	the Uttermost

Prayer Strategy

Education Strategy

Mission Strategy

Financial Strategy

Grow

Go

Give

Please complete one for yourself, or for your church. Sign and post in a visible place.

**Acts 1:8-Georgia
Challenge**

118

ACTS 1:8 PERFECT TEN PROFILE

A PROFILE

An Acts 1:8 CHRISTIAN
1. Saved and growing in Jesus
2. Deep desire to reach all people
3. A Biblical world view
4. Willing to be used of God
5. Flexible
6. Balanced in Mission
   - Involved in Jerusalem
   - Committed to Judea
   - Ready for Samaria
   - Excited about "the uttermost parts of the world"
7. Thinks Kingdom growth
8. Mission educated
9. Mission giver
10. Mission promoter

AN ACTS 1:8 CHURCH
1. Mission and evangelism centered
2. Budget reflects commitment to missions
3. Actively involved in many local mission works
4. At least one mission trip to Judea (state) offered each year
5. At least one mission trip to Samaria (the U.S.) offered each year
6. At least one world wide missions trip offered each year
7. A pastor committed to missions
8. A minister or a director of missions (paid or volunteer) or staff
9. A church committed to Kingdom growth
10 A healthy Kingdom church

AN ACTS 1:8 ASSOCIATION OF CHURCHES

1. A director of missions fully committed to Acts 1:8 missions
2. Provides local churches with missions leadership
3. Provide mission opportunities in each of the Acts 1:8 areas yearly
4. A growing library of mission materials available to local churches
5. Engaged in Partnership Missions
6. Often sponsors Mission Fairs, Mission Celebrations and Mission Outreaches
7. People driven
8. Cooperative in missions
9. Vision oriented
10. Mission Education

Partnership Missions Application

☐ Associational Team   Association Name: _____

☐ Church Team   Church Name: _____

☐ School Team   School Name: _____

☐ Individual   Name: _____

Mission Project Contact:

> The best way to reach me is: _____

_____
Name

_____
Address

_____
City   State   ZIP

_____
Home phone   Work phone   FAX

_____
E-mail address

Association/Church/School/Individual Address and Phone Number (*if different from above*):

_____

_____

_____

Dates available: 1. _____   2. _____   3. _____

Total number in group: _____

Breakdown of group by age: ____ Youth   ____ College   ____ Adults   ____ Senior Adults   ____ Other

How will you get to ministry site?
☐ Bus   ☐ Car   ☐ Van   ☐ Plane   ☐ Other: _____

What is your housing preference?
☐ Church   ☐ Homes   ☐ Hotel   ☐ Area Campus

—Application continued on back—

121

Partnership Missions Application (continued)

Our skills fit the following ministries:

☐ Children's Ministries
  __ VBS
  __ Backyard Bible Club

☐ Sports Clinics

☐ Block Party Assistance

☐ Performance Ministries
  __ Puppets
  __ Music
  __ Choir
  __ Drama
  __ Face Painting
  __ Clowning

☐ Special Event Ministries

☐ Campus/Student Outreach

☐ Renovation

☐ Inner-city Ministries

☐ Construction (list specific skills): ____
  _____
  _____
  _____

☐ Leadership Training Skills (please specify): _____
  _____
  _____

☐ Revival Team
  __ Preaching
  __ Survey
  __ Visitation

☐ Other: _____
  _____
  _____

Please describe any previous mission trip experience: _____
_____
_____
_____
_____

Please return form to: Mission Volunteers Ministries, Georgia Baptist Convention, 2930 Flowers Road South, Atlanta, GA 30341, or fax to (770) 452-6570. If you have questions, call (770) 936-5346.

For Office Use Only		
Placement Possibilities	**CALL** (date of, who called, talked with)	**RESULT**

Final Assignment: _____   Date: _____

Acts 1:8 Covenant

I, _____ covenant with God to become an Acts 1:8 Christian by prioritizing missions in my life through prayer, participation, education, and giving for my Jerusalem (city), my Judea (state), my Samaria (country), and the uttermost parts of the world

_____   _____
Signature   Date

_____   _____
Witness   Date

CHURCH PLANTING APPENDICES

APPENDIX 1

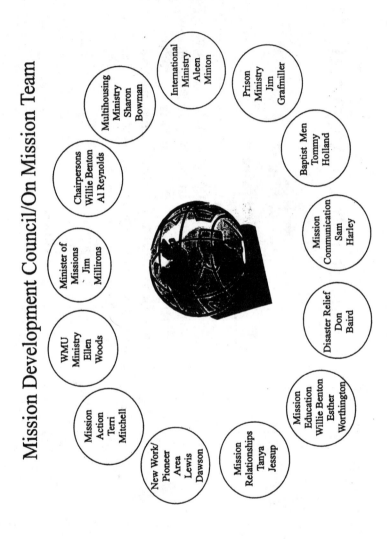

Mission Development Council/On Mission Team

International Ministry Aleen Minton

Prison Ministry Jim Grafmiller

Multihousing Ministry Sharon Bowman

Baptist Men Tommy Holland

Chairpersons Willie Benton Al Reynolds

Minister of Missions Jim Millirons

Mission Communication Sam Harley

WMU Ministry Ellen Woods

Disaster Relief Don Baird

Mission Action Terri Mitchell

New Work/Pioneer Area Lewis Dawson

Mission Relationships Tanya Jessup

Mission Education Willie Benton Esther Worthington

APPENDIX 2
Minister of Missions Job Description

The church Minister of Missions' basic job is to provide leadership for a church's missions ministries. This person reports directly to the senior pastor, and is responsible for leading in the development and implementation of comprehensive missions ministries. This involves discovering missions opportunities and developing a long-range plan with goals, strategies, and action plans. The church Minister of Missions oversees all ministries relating to the Church Missions Development Council, including enlisting, training, and supervising staff for needed ministries. The church Minister of Missions also supervises budget development and expenditures of budgeted and other funds.

Basic Job Assignment
1. Give general administration to the church's missions ministries.
2. Enlist and train leaders to staff all ministries.
3. Develop a total church evangelism planning strategy for the entire church and work to make every missions ministry evangelistic.
4. Give general administrative leadership to all missions trips.
5. Provide general supervision for all paid and volunteer staff.
6. Be a friend, consultant, and mentor to all mission/church pastors.
7. Supervise a reporting system that reflects accountability.
8. Work with leaders of churches, missions, indigenous satellite churches, and ministry programs to ensure that reports are made.
9. Work closely with project directors in planning, implementing, monitoring, and solving problems that relate to projects.
10. Work with pastors, projects directors, and other leaders in conducting growth reviews for all churches, missions, and indigenous satellite churches. Work with ministry staff; project directors; and associational, state convention, and NAMB leaders in church growth and effective reviews. Provide monthly reports as required on each project.
11. Respond positively to other assignments given by the pastor.

APPENDIX 3

On Mission Team Planning Sheet

Ministry Team _____

Priorities

1. _____ 4. _____

2. _____ 5. _____

3. _____

Goals

1A. _____ 1B. _____

2A _____ 2B. _____

3A. _____ 3B. _____

4A _____ 4B. _____

5A. _____ 5B. _____

6A. _____ 6B. _____

7A. _____ 7B. _____

8A _____ 8B. _____

9A. _____ 9B. _____

10A. _____ 10B. _____

Mission Project/Activity Dates

1. _____ 3. _____

2. _____ 4. _____

Budget Requests

1. _____ 4. _____

2. _____ 5. _____

3. _____

APPENDIX 4

Minister of Missions
Monthly Report

New Church Development
Georgia Baptist Convention
2930 Flowers Road South, Atlanta, GA 30341

Social Security #			Current Month		
Name			Chuch Name		
Home Mailing Address			Mailing Address		
City	State	Zip	City	State	Zip
Home Phone			Church Phone		
Work Phone			Fax/Email		
Fax/Email					

Church Growth Report

Did your MDC meet?

Current goals/plans for future missions/mission projects:

Current Mission Reporting

Mission/Ministry	*Relationship	Average Bible Study	Average Discipleship	Average Worship	Total Offering	Total Baptisms	Total New Members
1.							
2.							
3.							
4.							
5.							
6.							
7.							
8.							
9.							
10.							
Total							

Relationship 1 - Sponsoring Church   2 - Co-Sponsoring Church

Most Exciting Events:

Most Challenging Opportunities (Obstacles):

_____
Minister of Missions

_____
Superivsor

_____
State Convention

APPENDIX 5

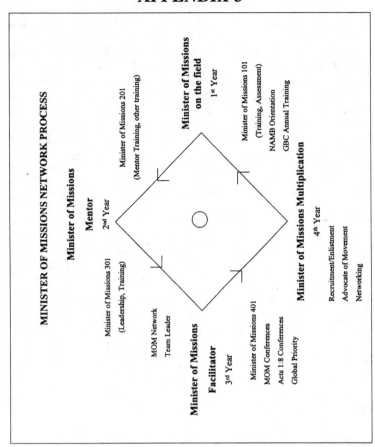

MINISTER OF MISSIONS NETWORK PROCESS

Minister of Missions
Mentor
2nd Year

Minister of Missions 201
(Mentor Training, other training)

Minister of Missions
on the field
1st Year

Minister of Missions 101
(Training, Assessment)
NAMB Orientation
GBC Annual Training

Minister of Missions 301
(Leadership, Training)

MOM Network
Team Leader

Minister of Missions
Facilitator
3rd Year

Minister of Missions 401
MOM Conferences
Acts 1:8 Conferences
Global Priority

Minister of Missions Multiplication
4th Year

Recruitment/Enlistment
Advocate of Movement
Networking

APPENDIX 6

Kinds of Churches

1. Mega Church

2. Meta Church

3. Community Church

4. Urban/Inner City Church

5. Neighborhood Church

6. Open -County Church

7. Multihousing Church

How Will Our Church Benefit From Key Church Strategy?

♦ KCS is a powerful tool of transforming lives with the gospel of Jesus Christ.

♦ KCS is a powerful way of expanding ministry with a focus on volunteers.

♦ KCS is a powerful method of building cooperation in a day that denominationalism is said to be in decline.

♦ KCS is a powerful strategy in revitalizing the self-centered or plateaued church.

(<u>Innovations in Ministry</u>, Lyle Schaller)

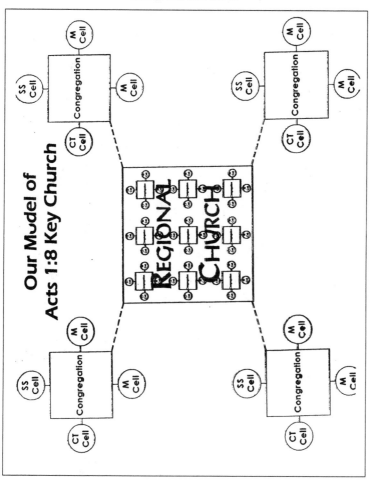

Our Model of
Acts 1:8 Key Church

PARTIAL BIBLIOGRAPHY OR SUGGESTED READING

Cogburn, Keith L., *Like the Book of Acts* (Franklin, Tennessee: Providence House Publishers, 1996).

Jones, J. Estell, *Acts: Working Together in Christ's Mission* (Nashville: Convention Press, 1974).

MacGoimans, J.W., *Acts: The Gospel for All People* (Nashville, Convention Press, 1998)

Stetzer, E.R., *Planting New Churches in a Post Modern Age* (Nashville: Broadman and Holman, 2003).

Vaughan, Curtis, *Acts: A Study Guide* (Grand Rapids: Zondervan, 1976).

White, J. Robert, *Healthy Kingdom Churches* (Friends Wood, Texas: Baxter Press, 2000).